ANGEL GANIVET

JUDITH GINSBERG

ANGEL GANIVET

TAMESIS BOOKS LIMITED
LONDON

Colección Támesis
SERIE A - MONOGRAFIAS, CXIII (113)

ISBN 0 7293 0203 2

Depósito legal: M. 12472-1985

Printed in Spain by Talleres Gráficos de Selecciones Gráficas
Carretera de Irún, km. 11,500. Madrid-34

for
TAMESIS BOOKS LIMITED
LONDON

To Paul, «*el ángel del hogar*»

CONTENTS

FOREWORD

Angel Ganivet —profound, complicated, strange, although virtually unknown to English readers— has fascinated, inspired and frustrated Spaniards since the publication of his *Idearium español* in 1897. One of the most representative literary spirits of his time, he was one of the first of the Generation of 1898 to express its patriotic concern over the character and future of a floundering nation. He also articulated the Generation's philosophic preoccupation with the existential anxieties of the individual, and in his last works he provided a meditation on artistic creativity.

The centennial of Ganivet's birth in 1965 gave rise to a series of studies which renewed interest in this key interpreter of Spain. *Papeles de Son Armadans, Revista de Occidente* and *Insula* all marked the occasion with essays on his life and works. Juan Agudiez, Antonio Gallego Morell, Javier Herrero, Miguel Olmedo Moreno, Herbert Ramsden and D. L. Shaw provided valuable new readings and insights into Ganivet studies and have salvaged many important letters and other documents that give us a clearer yet more complex picture of the personal and intelectual situation of the author.

The present study seeks to integrate further the works of these scholars and to provide several differing interpretations of Ganivet's life and works, to draw some connections that have not yet been drawn, and to point up a sense of humor in Ganivet that has been largely overlooked previously. Much attention has been granted to Ganivet's philosophical and religious conflicts, but insufficient account has been taken of his growing sense of himself as an artist and to his conception of art as a very broad activity, akin to charity in its moral quality and rather like the healing quality of a scar, which here emerges from a love that has not come to fruition.

What follows is conceived as a comprehensive account of this difficult and perplexing figure, who, while serving as a diplomat in foreign lands, composed, in addition to the *Idearium español,* two novels, one play, several collections of essays and over four volumes of correspondence. Chapter 1 discusses Ganivet's life in Granada, his birthplace, the years he spent in Madrid and his first academic and literary works. Chapters 2, 3, 4, 5, and 6 are arranged in chronological order and organized around the works that Ganivet completed during the remainder of his life. Each chapter concentrates on the work produced in a particular place

—Antwerp, Helsinki, Granada, Riga—and analyzes those works in the context in which they were written.

Unfortunately, any study of Ganivet must be hampered not only by the loss or destruction of many letters and documents but by the inaccessibility of other material, largely in the hands of Ganivet's family. Ganivet's *Obras completas* are far from complete, their organization arbitrary and confusing, and the bibliographic information given on the original publications in often inadequate. To offset such deficiencies this study provides a biographical Chronology and full Bibliography for all of Ganivet's published works as well as information on his projected works.

I would like to thank the Humanities Development Fund of Union College, Schenectady, New York, for its generous support of this project. My appreciation also goes to the helpful librarians at Union College and the Graduate School and University Center of the City University of New York. I am also grateful to Sara Schyfter, Rizel Sigele, and my husband for their invaluable comments on the manuscript and to Anne Goldstein for her excellent and patient typing of it.

ABBREVIATIONS

I or II	Volume number of Angel Ganivet's *Obras completas* (Madrid, Aguilar, 1961).
CFAG	*Correspondencia familiar de Angel Ganivet (1888-1897),* Javier Herrero, ed. (Granada, Anel, 1967).
GM:ET	Antonio Gallego Morell, *Estudios y textos ganivetianos* (Madrid, Consejo Superior de Investigaciones, 1971).
JA	Juan V. Agudiez, «Angel Ganivet y su correspondencia inédita con Francisco Navarro Ledesma,» *Nueva Revista de Filología Hispánica,* 21 (1972), 338-62.
	Javier Herrero, *Angel Ganivet, un iluminado* (Madrid, Gredos, 1966).
LSLP	Luis Seco de Lucena Paredes, *Juicio de Angel Ganivet sobre su obra literaria (cartas inéditas)* (Granada, Universidad de Granada, 1962).
NML	*La Cofradía del Avellano: Cartas de Angel Ganivet,* Nicolás María López, ed. (Granada, Luis F. Pinar Rocha, 1935).

CHAPTER 1

THE WRITER'S YOUTH IN SPAIN

Granada: the formative years

Angel Ganivet's brief, intense and unsettled life began in Granada on December 13, 1865. The second of six children of a family of millers, Ganivet remained lastingly devoted to his place of birth and to his hard-working yet artistically inclined parents. His father, Francisco Ganivet Morcillo, was a miller and an amateur artist who had served in the *Regimiento de Lanceros de Lusitania;* it was to this «artista y soldado,» as his son chose to remember him, that Ganivet dedicated his most famous work, *Idearium español,* in 1897.[1] Ganivet's mother, Angeles García Siles, the daughter of small mill owners, imparted her love of literature to her son; it was she who had always wanted him to be a writer, and as a man he much regretted that his mother had died before he had published anything significant.[2] Their relationship was a close one and he was to correspond faithfully with her, sharing the news of his academic and literary progress from the time he first left Granada in 1888 until her death in 1895.[3]

Little is known about Ganivet's earliest years since his writings touch on them but lightly. He seems to have occupied his days like other young boys of his age and class in Granada. He recalled skipping meetings of the Congregation of San Luis Gonzaga to play with friends flying kites, participating in make-believe bull fights, and collecting a series of playing cards reproduced on the back of match boxes. In «Una derrota de los greñudos,» published posthumously in the collection

[1] ANGEL GANIVET, *Obras completas* (Madrid, 1961), I, 147-305. Subsequent references to Ganivet's *Obras completas* will be abbreviated in parentheses in the text, the volume indicated by a roman numeral followed by the pages in arabic numerals.

[2] NICOLÁS MARÍA LÓPEZ, *La Cofradía del Avellano: Cartas de Angel Ganivet* (Granada, 1935), 82. Subsequent references to this volume will be abbreviated in parentheses in the text as NML, followed by the page number.

[3] Many of these letters are in JAVIER HERRERO (ed.), *Correspondencia familiar de Angel Ganivet: 1888-1897* (Granada, 1967). Subsequent references from this work will be abbreviated in parentheses in the text as CFAG, followed by the page number. Often, in letters to his mother, Ganivet would note her spelling mistakes and offer corrections, indicative of his superior educational level and his desire to help her.

Libro de Granada, Ganivet colorfully describes a battle between boys of the parish of San Cecilio and those of las Angustias in which he received a head injury. Here he captures the freewheeling spirit of the event, the feel of a young boy's Granada, and the rivalry between the hillside dwellers, the *greñudos,* and those who lived on the flat plains.

Although sketchy, Ganivet's reports of these early years disclose traces of the future author's character. An often cited anecdote about the theft of the young Ganivet's cap at a religious procession contains the first indication of what was to become one of Ganivet's more notable qualities, a unique generosity of spirit. When his mother asked him why he had not screamed for a policeman to pursue the thief, Ganivet calmly explained: «Pensé que a él le haría más falta que a mí».[4]

Another characteristic traceable to this period is Ganivet's ability to form close and lasting friendships with his teachers. As early as elementary school Ganivet began forming enduring ties with those who taught him. One teacher of these first years, Don Francisco Casares, remained a close friend until Ganivet's death. Another teacher from secondary school and yet another from the University of Granada enjoyed the same kind of devotion from their pupil.[5]

This period also provides incidents that may have contributed to the emotional instability that characterized Ganivet's last weeks. A few months before Ganivet's tenth birthday on September 4, 1875, his father died of stomach cancer at the age of 41. The family, which had been spending the summer in the small town of Dúdar, returned to Granada and moved into the home of Ganivet's maternal grandfather at the *Molino de Sagra* on the Cuesta de Molinos, a hill leading up to the Alhambra with an imposing view of its towers. The fatherless boy now came under the powerful influence of his mother's father, Francisco de Paula García Hurtado, who assumed responsibility for his daughter's family until he was struck by paralysis three years later.

Although Ganivet eventually frustrated his grandfather's plans for him to succeed him in the flour trade, he considered the mill where he lived for thirteen years to be his true «home» for the rest of his life, even though he left Granada permanently in 1888. «Tú me has corregido muchas veces cuando decía *la casa* por casa o mi casa,» he wrote to a friend in 1893, «y a pesar de la corrección continúo y creo que continuaré siempre, aunque llegara a habitar un palacio de mi propiedad llamando *mi casa* al molino de Granada, y la casa a cualquiera otra que habite, aquí o en Chicago» (II, 1001). Indeed, despite the extent of his future travels —extraordinary for a Spaniard of his time—and his prolonged residence abroad, Ganivet never overcame the nostalgia for the idealized Granada

[4] Antonio Gallego Morell, *Angel Ganivet: el excéntrico del 98* (Madrid, 1974), 12.

[5] Testimony to the longevity of these early relationships are the letters Ganivet wrote to his teachers in adult life. Two have been published: «Dos cartas inéditas de Angel Ganivet,» *Anales de la Facultad de Filosofía y Letras,* Universidad de Granada, No. 2 (1926), 107-11.

of his childhood, which may also have been a nostalgia for the emotional security of his first years.

Another incident of this time exhibits Ganivet's tenacity, energy and willpower. Early in 1876 a serious fracture from a fall badly shattered Ganivet's leg, and should have required amputation. The boy hovered for a while between life and death, but once out of mortal danger he adamantly refused to allow the amputation. He subsequently spent several months in bed while his mother nursed him affectionately and conscientiously and at considerable cost. When able to rise at last, he had a limp which seemed certain to be permanent. But, refusing to use crutches and by sheer force of will, he overcame the limp. As a permanent reminder of this triumph Ganivet kept a few bits of shattered bone, neatly preserved in one of the match boxes he loved to collect. The time spent convalescing gave the boy his first opportunity to read uninterruptedly and his intellectual curiosity was awakened. Yet a special dependence on mother and home was created, since he spent much time alone with her while his siblings were out of the house and for almost ten consecutive years following this event she would take him to the sulphur baths in Jaén.[6] Her name for him «mi niño de oro» seems to have referred not only to the enormous emotional attachment she had for this child, but to the financial investment that had been made in his recuperation as well.[7] His withdrawal from most social life as an adult may also have had its roots in the habits developed during this period. Herrero has observed that between mother and son «probablemente se estableció... esa especial intimidad que hace que Angel se considere siempre espiritualmente dependiente de su hogar granadino.»[8]

All told, Ganivet spent some three years overcoming his injury, displaying a tenacity for life all the more remarkable, as Joaquín Casalduero points out, when this youthful will to live and overcome is set against Ganivet's emotional situation twenty-two years later, when, in a desperate renunciation of life, he drowned himself in the Dvina River in Riga.[9]

As a consequence of his illness, Ganivet fell behind in school, and he quit at the age of twelve to work in the *notaría* of Abelardo Martínez Contreras. There he demonstrated such intelligence that Don Francisco Guerrero, one of the partners, advised his mother that he should continue his education. His former elementary school teacher,

[6] Gallego Morell, *Angel Ganivet...*, 15.

[7] This special attachment between mother and son also characterized the relationship between Ganivet's contemporary, Sigmund Freud, and his mother. Ernest Jones, *The Life and Work of Sigmund Freud* (New York, 1961), 4, comments: «It was strange to a young visitor to hear her [Freud's mother] refer to the great master as *'mein goldener Sigi'* and evidently there was throughout a close attachment between the two.»

[8] Javier Herrero, *Angel Ganivet, un iluminado* (Madrid, 1966), 22. Future references to this volume will be abbreviated in parentheses in the text as JH followed by the page number.

[9] Joaquín Casualduero, «El problema de la muerte en Ganivet,» *Estudios de literatura española* (Madrid, 1962), 147-8.

Don Francisco Casares, helped him prepare for the high school entrance exam, which he passed in June of 1880. He matriculated the following fall and began a distinguished academic career.

As a student at the Instituto de Granada, Ganivet studied the usual fare of the times: Latin, Spanish, French, Geography, World History, Rhetoric, Poetics, Algebra, Psychology, Logic, Ethics, Geometry, Trigonometry, Physics, Chemistry, Physiology, Hygiene, and Elementary Agriculture.

As if to make up for lost time, Ganivet put all his energies into finishing his secondary education with distinction, graduating in five years with outstanding grades, and receiving the *premio extraordinario* and a prestigious scholarship to support further studies. But if he was an able student, he was not always a model one. Two anecdotes particularly illustrate his difficulty in accepting male authority as an adolescent, perhaps the result of the lack of such authority in his own home given his father's death and his grandfather's paralysis. Ganivet himself recalled years later that in school he would be overcome by more or less sardonic laughter when confronted with the «principio de autoridad»: just seeing a teacher's cat-o-nine-tails or a professor lecturing from on high could prompt an outburst, and the punishments for his lack of decorum would make him laugh all the more. He could only contain himself, he said, by thinking of all the people he knew who had died, starting with his father (II, 814). And although his translation, in 1881, of the story of Judith from Latin into Spanish may have been Ganivet's first literary work, a high school classmate, Francisco Seco de Lucena, recalls an incident in which Ganivet set definite limits to his tolerance for verbal busywork. When the rhetoric teacher once gave the class ten words with which to end each of the ten lines of a Spanish *décima* and asked them to make up the rest, Angel refused to do the assignment, asserting that instead of writing nonsense in verse, one should write in prose, or, as he himself did, not write at all.[10]

Ganivet recalled in 1893 that when studying rhetoric at the Instituto he had begun to read the works of Lope de Vega in the Rivadeneyra Collection, and, dreaming of becoming a theatre critic in a local newspaper, he hoped—with a certain malice—to be able to unmask fashionable playwrights as plagiarists of the great Lope. But clearly the author who influenced him most during these years was Seneca. Indeed, for Ganivet senequism, with its belief in man's integrity and the limitations of material existence, is the axis of the Hispanic character.[11] In the *Idearium* he describes the enormous impact the first reading of this stoic philosopher produced on him: «Cuando yo, siendo estudiante, leí las obras de Séneca, me quedé aturdido y asombrado, como quien, perdida la vista o el oído los recobrara repetina e inesperadamente y viera los objetos, que con sus

[10] LUIS SECO DE LUCENA PAREDES, *Juicio de Angel Ganivet sobre su obra literaria* (Granada, 1954), 8-10. Future references to this volume will be abbreviated in parentheses in the text as LSLP followed by the page number.

[11] See MANUEL DURÁN, «Ganivet y el senequismo hispánico,» *Insula*, 228-9, November-December (1965), 3, 9.

colores y sonidos ideales se agitaban antes confusos en su interior, salir ahora en tropel y tomar la consistencia de objetos reales y tangibles» (I, 152-3).

In the fall of 1885, Ganivet matriculated in both the Law and Arts Faculties at the University of Granada, although his enthusiasm for legal studies was minimal. «Yo he estudiado leyes,» he said later, «y no he podido ser abogado porque jamás llegué a ver el mecanismo judicial por su lado noble y serio» (I, 202).[12]

Several of the friendships Ganivet formed at the University were to be lifelong, even though his years in Granada ended in 1888 and he visited only occasionally thereafter. Important among those friends were the distinguished Professor of Greek, Don Antonio González Barbín, whom Ganivet described to Unamuno as the man «que más había contribuido a formar su espíritu,»[13] and Francisco Seco de Lucena. It was through Seco de Lucena that Ganivet became associated with the local newspaper, *El Defensor de Granada.* Seco de Lucena's brother Luis, an editor of the paper, invited Ganivet to contribute several pieces, but at first the future author of *Idearium español* declined, preferring to spend his energies on his studies in law and arts as well as beginning German classes three times a week. *El Defensor,* nonetheless, was where Ganivet first chose to publish much of his work when he later started writing seriously.

According to a friend and classmate of the time, Manuel Gómez Moreno, with whom Ganivet studied Greek every day at his mill in the summer of 1887, Ganivet's appearance during this period was hardly elegant. He had a Lincoln-style beard but no moustache, giving him the look of a coachman. His heavy-set shoulders, weak nose with its squashed bridge, and a slight prognathism, gave him a certain simian air. He was quite heavy and smoked cigars continually. He carried a walking stick which at times he tapped on the ground like a blind man. But he had light eyes, a sweet, penetrating gaze, and «su sonrisa inalterable atraía como transparentando limpieza de alma.»[14] Others noted in Ganivet's physical appearance a certain peculiarity, bordering on mystery. Even Ganivet noticed a strangeness in people's reactions to him, although, as he told his mother, it could take the rather unexalted form of his being judged a stranger and mistaken for a traveling salesman (CFAG, 43). Francisco Navarro Ledesma, a fellow student Ganivet met in 1888-89 and who was to become his intimate friend and fervent champion, described him as striking so «unique» a figure that «sobre unos y otras sin querer y sin darse cuenta y sin hablar palabra, ejercía inexplicable e imperioso influjo, tal como debieron ejercerle todos los precursores y todos los Mesías.»[15]

[12] Other negative comments on the legal profession are found in II, 852, 988.

[13] MIGUEL DE UNAMUNO, *Contra esto y aquello* (Madrid, 1912), 219-20.

[14] MANUEL GÓMEZ MORENO, «Recuerdos de un condiscípulo,» *Revista de Occidente* III, no. 33 (1965), 327.

[15] FRANCISCO NAVARRO LEDESMA, «Prólogo,» *Epistolario de Angel Ganivet,* Madrid, 1904, 14. See CARMEN DE ZULUETA, *Navarro Ledesma, el hombre y su*

Madrid: failures and successes

After receiving his degree in Arts as well as winning the *Premio Extraordinario* in 1888, Ganivet moved to Madrid at the beginning of the academic year 1888-89 to pursue a doctorate while finishing up work for his law degree. He received his doctorate in Philosophy and Letters in early 1890, and obtained his law degree in June of the same year. In the spring of 1889, motivated by the desire to cease being a financial burden to his family and encouraged by Navarro Ledesma and another son of Granada, his lifelong friend Nicolás María López, Ganivet followed the common route of ambitious but politically and financially unconnected young men who aspired to permanent state positions: he took the *oposiciones* for a position as a Government archivist. He placed eleventh in the exam, and in the early summer he was assigned to the *Biblioteca Agrícola* of the Ministerio de Fomento.

Enjoying the financial independence that his new position brought, Ganivet briefly visited Granada to disclaim, in favor of his sisters, any rights he had to his mother's and father's estate. His reasons for this are clear in a letter he wrote to his family a few years later on the topic of family finances: «Si me alegro de las prosperidades de la casa,» he explained, "es por los demás, no por mí, que con mis estudios he sacado ya mi parte por anticipado» (CFAG, 210). This was but another instance of the generosity, both physical and spiritual, and the true disdain for property that marked Ganivet's character from childhood to death.[16] His friends revered him for it, and many of them benefitted directly, for he gave readily of his energies and learning, tutoring and helping them prepare for exams. He even taught the maid of the first boarding house where he lived in Madrid to read and write.[17]

Ganivet's pleasure over obtaining a position as a librarian was somewhat dampened in the spring of 1889 when the chair of his doctoral committee, Don Nicolás Salmerón, rejected his first doctoral thesis, *España filosófica contemporánea.* This work, an analysis of what the not yet twenty-four year old student perceived as Spain's intellectual state, brought about by the absence of *ideas madres,* positive vital convictions, prefigures in particular Ganivet's later investigation of Spain and her goals in the *Idearium.* Although critics have pointed out the vague and naive nature of the educational remedy Ganivet proposed to stem the crisis of skepticism in which his country wavered, D. L. Shaw finds this dissertation «unequalled» as a «diagnosis of the causes and effects of the general breakdown of confidence which underlies the sensibility of the Generation of 1898.»[18].

tiempo (Madrid-Barcelona, 1968) for a comprehensive study of Ganivet's closest friend.

[16] See JH, 20-38 for a fuller consideration of this fundamental aspect of his character.

[17] This maid appears as Purilla in Ganivet's novel *Los trabajos del infatigable creador, Pío Cid*; see below, 86-82. See also Nicolás María López, *Viajes románticos de Antón del Sauce* (Granada, no date), 32.

[18] «Ganivet's *España filosófica contemporánea* and the Interpretation of the

España filosófica is also significant as the earliest formulation of Ganivet's *ars poetica,* one which notably emphasizes the philosophical basis of literature, and his first mention of the influence readers can have on authors.[19] Here Ganivet states that:

> ... el público no es sencillamente un lector, sino un elemento activo, porque su censura o aplauso, ya sean inmediatos, directos y colectivos, como acontece en las representaciones escénicas, ya mediatos, indirectos e individuales, como en la poesía o en la novela, influyen decisivamente sobre el artista y lo impulsan por el camino emprendido o lo detienen. (I, 602)

Nine years later, when he sent his play *El escultor de su alma* to Granada, he expressed essentially the same idea, hoping that the audience's response to his work would guide him and others in future theatrical efforts.

In *España filosófica* Ganivet also signals the value of popular poetry:

> El pueblo no escribe, pero canta, y sus cantares fueron siempre la expresión llena de vida, sencilla, poética, de sus aspiraciones, sentimientos y creencias, y la más acabada epopeya nacional. (II, 602)

Although these views were shared by critics all over Europe at the time, the similarity of these lines to Bécquer's poetics is particularly striking:

> El pueblo ha sido, y será siempre, el gran poeta de todas las edades y de todas las naciones. Nadie mejor que él sabe sintetizar en sus obras las creencias, las aspiraciones y el sentimiento de una época.[20]

Bécquer appears to be a more important influence on Ganivet than has been previously noted, an influence that is also apparent in the pieces Ganivet contributed to the posthumous *Libro de Granada* (1899).

Ganivet was undeterred by the failure of his first thesis, however, and he prepared another one during the summer. «*Importancia de la lengua sánscrita y servicios que su estudio ha prestado a la ciencia del lenguaje en general y a la gramática comparada en particular,*» which was accepted in the fall of 1889 and in which the significance of national character, an important theme of Ganivet's in later years, is explicit. Here Ganivet finds the study of language to be the prime field of inquiry among many leading to an understanding of the character and genius of each nation (II, 868).[21] Ganivet was to follow this view for the rest of his

Generation of 1898,» *Hispanic Review,* XXVIII (1960), 221. See also K. E. Shaw, «Angel Ganivet: A Sociological Interpretation,» *Revista de Estudios Hispánicos,* II (1968): 170-3.

[19] Andrés Soria, «Ganivet, el escritor,» *Insula,* 228-9 (1965), 11, provides a brief consideration of some of Ganivet's writings on literature.

[20] Gustavo Adolfo Bécquer, *Rimas,* José Luis Cano, ed. (Salamanca, Anaya, 1965), 23. Antonio Machado, *Antología poética,* would share these views, but Juan Ramón Jiménez in his *Segunda antología poética,* would differ sharply.

[21] John P. Wonder, «Angel Ganivet and the Study of Languages,» *Romance Notes* 11 (1969), 82-8, offers a positive evaluation of Ganivet's scholarship in this dissertation.

life and he learned all the widely spoken languages of Europe and used them to understand the culture of foreign nations.

In his second dissertation Ganivet also indicates his understanding of the «new» conception of history in which the chronological narration of facts has been replaced by «la exposición de los acontecimientos que constituyen la vida de los pueblos en cada forma transitoria de una misma esencia, el linaje humano, y enlazadas estrechamente por las leyes de la *generación,* de la *solidaridad* y del *progreso*» (I, 867-8). It is largely this conception of history and its concern for a nation's «interior life» which underlies the *Idearium,* written seven years later.

Several months after the acceptance of «Importancia de la lengua sánscrita,» he gained further academic recognition by winning the *Premio Extraordinario,* awarded with the doctorate for an essay written in four hours, as stipulated by the academic procedures of the time, and entitled «Doctrinas varias de los filósofos sobre el concepto de causa y verdadero origen y subjetivo valor de ese concepto.»

In a letter written to Navarro Ledesma in 1890, not long after this, Ganivet confides that he is:

> ... aburrido, hastiado, malhumorado, melancólico, abrumado, entontecido... creo que es todo eso junto y algo más.
>
> Y quizás sea por faltarme las creencias. ¿Sabes tú si los creyentes no están nunca abroncados? Porque entonces yo creería en algo aunque me costase trabajo, pues en verdad te digo, que con este escepticismo, nada, que no puede uno estar tranquilo.[22]

Here is one of the earliest indications of Ganivet's personal distress and it is interesting to note the correspondence between his own internal situation and his analysis of Spain's intellectual state in *España filosófica.* Herbert Ramsden has most effectively demonstrated a similar correspondence between Ganivet's perceptions of his interior state and his interpretation of Spain in the *Idearium.*[23]

In a letter written to Navarro Ledesma in 1890, not long after this, discovered in the late 1920's by the German scholar Hans Jeschke among Ganivet's son's papers, was probably also written during the period that the author was studying in Madrid.[24] This piece also provides insight into Ganivet's tormented character and his later art. The unnamed protagonist, probably the first in a series of autobiographical incarnations, suffers from an acute «skeptic infection» and is enraged by the spectacle of Spanish life that he encounters on a walk. He is sadistic and suicidal «¡Creo en la desesperación suicida y en el odio al linaje humano!» (JH, 284). At nightfall, however, his nature is transformed. He muses that,

[22] JUAN AGUDIEZ, «Angel Ganivet y su correspondencia inédita con Francisco Navarro Ledesma,» *Nueva Revista de Filología Hispánica,* XXI (1974), 334-56. Future references to this article will be abbreviated in parentheses in the text as JA followed by the page number.

[23] See HERBERT RAMSDEN, *Angel Ganivet's 'Idearium español': A Critical Study* (Manchester, 1967), 150-3.

[24] JH, 284-90, not in the *Obras.*

perhaps during a profound lethargy experienced by his body, his mind has immersed itself in the «universal spirit» purifying itself of its miseries and has returned to its worthless abode, bringing with it peace and joy. After this experience, the character's patriotic pride is aroused by what previously disgusted him and he is kindly disposed toward his less fortunate fellow creatures.

The conflicting arrogance and grandiosity, as seen in the title, «Yo soy el mundo», and the character's initial behavior and reactions and the mystical oneness with humanity seen in his later actions are paradigmatic for both Ganivet and the future heroes of his fiction, Pío Cid and Pedro Mártir. Herrero, the first to republish this article and give it the critical attention it deserves, finds in it a compendium of Ganivet's most significant traits:

> En realidad, tenemos ahí, en síntesis, todos los elementos que lo caracterizan: rebelión frente a una realidad injusta... abulia y «desesperación suicida»; furor destructor del idealista frente a la miseria de lo real; éxtasis en que el espíritu se une al ser trascendente..., y vuelto ahora el ánimo a un mundo envuelto en sombras (una idea básica de Ganivet...) una simpatía universal por todo, hombres y cosas, que descubre en lo más miserable lo bello que lo ennoblece...» (JH, 58)

Further material important for an appreciation of Ganivet's student writing has been discovered by Juan Agudiez, who has found several interesting sketches and poems as well as some of Ganivet's statements on art in the Ganivet-Navarro correspondence of this period. In September of 1891 Ganivet insisted that the artist must not only arrange the artistic elements of a work into a whole; he must fuse them if he wishes to create something beautiful. Even if the artist's personality is disjointed, he must strive to overcome his own limitations because «las palabras arte e irreflexión o espontaneidad son incompatibles.» For Ganivet, at this time, spontaneity had its place in only two circumstances: in expressions of the spirit free of artistic pretensions and in life, which is «un arte espontáneo» (JA, 346).

The following week Ganivet continued in the same vein and stated his admiration of originality, an admiration that was to be life-long: «Reverencio a todos los iniciadores y soy fatalmente enemigo de seguir los caminos trillados, cuando hay otros por donde se vaya a alguna parte» (JA, 346).

His student writings and aesthetic concerns, however, did not provide him with a livelihood. Bored by his position as a librarian, Ganivet sought greater professional satisfaction and economic rewards. When the competitive exams for a chair in Greek at the University of Granada were opened in June of 1891, he was among the contestants. Although he failed to win the chair, the exams brought him a new and important friend: Miguel de Unamuno. Unamuno was competing at the same time for the chair in Greek at the University of Salamanca. And he succeeded. But while the two contestants never met again after the exam, the friendship born in those weeks was to bear important fruit, for Ganivet and Unamuno later exchanged letters on Spain's cultural and political problems in the wake of her defeat by the United States in 1898. This correspondence, first published in *El Defensor de Granada* and later in book form as *El porvenir de España,* was to be a prime document of the Generation of '98.[25]

Despite the new friendship, Ganivet was stung by his failure to win the Greek chair at Granada, his first major academic setback. His later references to the incident, in letters and other works, are tinged with a resentment that carried over into his feelings toward the teaching profession in general.[26] In 1893 he complained to his mother from Antwerp that the examinations were clearly not designed to reward the highest expertise in Greek. But, he concluded, perhaps this was a benefit in disguise because «creo que ni enseñando bien ni mal se adelanta nada» (CFAG, 136). And in a letter to Navarro Ledesma, he wonders how anyone could love Homer after analyzing and translating him every day in class—it would be like being married to the Venus de Milo (II, 878).

Finding the pathway to teaching temporarily blocked, Ganivet set his sights on a new profession. In early 1892, the dissatisfied librarian with a law degree and a doctorate became a clerk in the law office of Don Joaquín López Puigcerver, a former Liberal Minister specializing in financial and administrative matters. At about the same time, Ganivet began preparing for the competitive exams, given in April and May, to enter the diplomatic corps as a vice consul. He succeeded grandly. Placing first in the field of aspirants, he was appointed to the post of Spanish Vice Consul in Antwerp, Belgium, where he moved in the early summer. Old defeats were pushed aside. A new life was beginning. Happier to leave his librarian position than to assume his diplomatic post, he nonetheless saw his new career as an opportunity to study books and languages under improved conditions (CFAG, 86). Unlike many who gain a secure position for the sake of ease, the new vice consul embraced his appointment as a chance for self-improvement.

The first half of 1892 was a pivotal time in Ganivet's life. In addition to securing a permanent professional position, his personal life underwent a profound change. While a student in Madrid he had probably had his first sexual encounters; it was then that he might have contracted the syphilis that appears to have been responsible for the insanity of his last days and which well may have contributed to his suicide.[27] But in February, 1892, in the unlikely setting of a carnival, he fell in love for the first time. This episode, as well as a number of other autobiographi-

[25] GALLEGO MORELL, *Ganivet...*: 162.

[26] In the satiric novel, *La conquista del reino de Maya por el último conquistador español, Pío Cid,* teaching competence, for example, is demonstrated by training parrots.

[27] LEOPOLDO ROMEO, a friend of Ganivet's in Madrid, commented on his occasional absences from his circle of friends, alleging that he was somewhat of a womanizer (JH, 54.5, Herrero also cites here the opinion of Dr. G. M. Carstairs that Ganivet's symptoms were of syphilitic origin). C. Castilla del Pino, «Para una patografía de Angel Ganivet,» *Insula,* 228-9 (1965), 5, is skeptical of this diagnosis while stressing that Ganivet suffered from severe depression.

cal incidents which shed light on Ganivet's Madrid experiences, appears in his novel *Los trabajos del infatigable creador, Pío Cid.* In the story, the romantic meeting occurs at a masked ball. Smitten by love at first sight, Pío Cid-Ganivet immediately assumes financial responsibility for the impoverished young woman and her family, and considers her his *de facto,* if not *de jure* wife. The Martina of Pío Cid was in life Amelia Roldán Llanos.

Roldán was born in Valencia in 1868. Her father, a Cuban, had died quite young and she and her mother had lived for a while in Barcelona before moving to Madrid where she met Ganivet. According to contemporary accounts she was a beautiful woman with extraordinary dark eyes and a lovely singing voice.[28] From the time of their meeting until his death in 1898, the two lived together intermittently in Madrid, Antwerp and Helsinki, although they never married. They had two children: Natalia, born in December of 1893, lived only a few months; and Angel Tristán, born in November of 1894. However nourished it may have been on love, the relationship appears to have known many troubles. The details of their life together are unfortunately lost to us. Ganivet's closest confidants, Francisco Navarro Ledesma and Nicolás María López, maintained a discreet silence about whatever secrets they knew, the latter apparently having possessed some of Ganivet's letters containing the most explicit material on his affair with Roldán. Moreover, the loss of almost all the Ganivet-Roldán correspondence permanently shrouds the tortured but lasting love affair in darkness. The nature of their commitment to each other was ambiguous, but enduring. Although «Alter ego,» as Ganivet sometimes referred to Roldán, was apparently unfaithful to him, he was also unfaithful to her and admitted to several infidelities.[29]. Nonetheless, just two days before his death he summed up the loves of his life: «He tenido varios amoríos y un amor más noble a Amelia, a la que he dado muy malos ratos con mis necedades.»[30].

Ganivet's meeting with Roldán and his subsequent career change brought to a close the author's years in Spain. Intellectually, Ganivet profited enormously from his stay in Madrid. At the University, as Herrero has pointed out, he came into contact with a number of professors who were *Krausistas.* Their influence is apparent particularly in the conception of education embodied by Pío Cid in *Los trabajos del infatigable creador, Pío Cid.* At the *Ateneo,* the center of intellectual life in the capital, he found the only society in Spain to his liking—tolerant and wide ranging, yet with the certain warmth and unity of an intellectual

[28] There are several photographs of her, Ganivet, and other relevant figures in Antonio Gallego Morell, *Estudios y textos ganivetianos* (Madrid, 1971), *passim.* Future references to this work will be abbreviated in parentheses in the text as GM: ET followed by the page number. There is also a photograph of her with Angel Tristán, the son she bore Ganivet, *Insula,* 228-9 (1965), 5.

[29] See JH, 9-10, 25, 27, 31 and also Gallego Morell, *Angel Ganivet...,* 55-7, and Juan Agudiez, *Las novelas de Angel Ganivet* (New York, 1972), 34-6. See also JA, 334-56, which adds valuable information to our knowledge of the Ganivet-Roldán liaison.

[30] «Epistolario,» *Revista de Occidente,* II (1965), 323.

community.[31] Ganivet, already somewhat misanthropic, wrote to his mother from Madrid in early 1892 that, if it were not for the gatherings at the *Ateneo,* he would remain as solitary as a hermit in the capital, and he cited approvingly the Spanish proverb, «Mejor solo que mal acompañado.» In Madrid Ganivet also established a pattern of disciplined and rigourous intellectual effort, reading voraciously—often from 8 in the evening to past midnight (CFAG, 51)—in publications of both the national and foreign press, novels, notably those of Juan Valera, criticism (e. g., Sainte-Beuve's *Causeries du lundi*), philosophy, history, and travel books. As Andrés Soria has commented, «Ganivet—como Unamuno—son lectores: pocos casos como los suyos, en el mundo de nuestras letras de la bibliofagia, de la lectura como alimento.»[32] A corollary to this «biblofagia» and a logical complement to it, would be his own extraordinary literary production over the next six years.

[31] GALLEGO MORELL, *Angel Ganivet,* 55. For a description of the Madrid Athenaeum in the nineteenth century see Antonio Ruiz Salvador, *El Ateneo Científico, Literario y Artístico de Madrid,* 1835-1885 (London, 1971).
[32] ANDRÉS SORIA, «Ganivet, el escritor,» *Insula,* 228-9 (1965), 11.

CHAPTER 2

ANTWERP

When Angel Ganivet took up his post as Spanish Vice Consul in Antwerp on July 11, 1892, he was embarking upon two new but related careers—one diplomatic, the other literary. The first, which made him a voluntary exile in the service of his country for the next six years, not only provided him a livelihood but exposed him to the vigorous cultural life of Europe; the second gave him a means of exploring that cultural life as well as of probing the character and problems of his homeland and himself, and it gave him an impressive, although largely posthumous, reputation.

The three and a half years Ganivet spent in Belgium saw the beginnings of this reputation with his first publications, several articles written for *El Defensor de Granada* («Un festival literario en Amberes,»[1] «Lecturas extranjeras,» «Arte gótico,» and «Socialismo y música»)[2] and the composition of his novel, *La conquista del reino de Maya por el último conquistador español, Pío Cid* (first printed at the author's expense in Madrid in April of 1897). But despite this budding literary life, Ganivet's Belgian years were not happy ones. Although he appears to have been an honest, able, and dedicated official, whose work was routinely approved by the consul, Ganivet did not enjoy his diplomatic responsibilities, and his personal life was marred by betrayal and tragedy. And although he took advantage of the cultural and intellectual opportunities afforded him in Antwerp, he found little to admire in the Belgians and their culture. He was often painfully aware of being in an alien environment whose growing mechanization and commercialization he detested.

The troubles began shortly after his arrival in Antwerp when he received word that his mistress, Amelia Roldán, who had remained in Barcelona ill with typhus, had been unfaithful to him. After recovering from the disease, she arrived (probably in November), asking his for-

[1] This appeared August 21, 1892, and is his first extant published work. Letters to his family, however, indicate that before 1892 he sent a number of chronicles to Navarro Ledesma for publication in his ephemeral newspaper *El Heraldo,* which was published until the spring of 1893 (CFAG, 119).

[2] «Lecturas extranjeras,» October 4, 1895; «Arte gótico,» November 17, 1895; «Socialismo y música,» November 23, 1895.

giveness—the first of many such requests.[3] But the damage was done. For although Ganivet admitted to several flirtations of his own in Antwerp, he was deeply disillusioned by Amelia's infidelity and this made him increasingly critical of women in general.[4] Comments disparaging women and marriage regularly appear in his correspondence from Antwerp (II, 840-2; 859-61; 989; CFAG, 32, 46). Shortly after the discovery, for instance, Ganivet complained that «no hay tales mujeres finas y delicadas... La finura y delicadeza de la mujer consiste en la distancia a que nos ponemos y se desvanecen según nos acercamos» (JA, 353). Later, while in Belgium, he seems to have become so disillusioned with the opposite sex that he concluded that an honorable man's only recourse was to do as Don Quixote had done with Aldonza Lorenzo:

> tomar de ella la «idea de sexo» nada más... y reconstruir sobre este pequeño cimiento un castillo imaginario que llegue hasta donde se pueda. Dentro de ese castillo es donde únicamente puede habitar la señora de nuestros pensamientos, la que nos inspire un amor que sea algo distinto del usual y corriente entre los animales. (II, 971)

But for all his disillusionment with «Alter ego,» as Ganivet called her in fonder moments, he did not give her up. Indeed, she and her mother joined him in the Belgian port where, to preserve appearances, he supported the two women in a separate residence, and at considerable cost. In December of 1893 Amelia bore him a daughter, Natalia, named after Ganivet's brother Natalio who had died of tuberculosis in 1889. But the child was even less fortunate than her namesake, for she died of meningitis just two months after her birth and while in the care of a wet nurse in the village of Saint Léger les Domart, near Amiens. It is likely, as Gallego Morell asserts, that Ganivet never forgave Amelia for entrusting the care of their daughter to a stranger but, on the other hand, the child's mother may well have found the prospect of caring for an illegitimate infant in a foreign city quite overwhelming and the practice of entrusting infants to wet nurses was well accepted at the time.[5]

Although he hardly saw Natalia, Ganivet was deeply touched by the loss of this child. Almost two years later, in a macabre episode on All Souls Day of 1895 he visited her grave, had the body exhumed and, in a sentimental gesture, placed the portraits of her parents and her unseen brother, Angel Tristán, beside her lifeless head.[6]

In November of 1894, Amelia again gave birth, this time to a son, Angel Tristán. Like the short-lived Natalia, Angel was born in Paris

[3] Gallego Morell, *Angel Ganivet...*, 79.

[4] See II, 970, and JA, 353-4.

[5] *Angel Ganivet...*, 94. See Elizabeth Badinter's iconoclastic and controversial *Mother Love: Myth and Reality* (New York, 1981) for an analysis of the custom in France.

[6] GM:ET, 158-60 reproduces Ganivet's letter of November 3, 1895, to Roldán in which he describes this episode.

where the parents had journeyed to avoid registering the illegitimate births at the Spanish consulate in Antwerp. Ganivet's loathing of marriage necessitated the inconvenience. Nor did Ganivet look on fatherhood with any more hope and affection than he viewed marriage and the rest of life. Just a month after Angel's birth, Ganivet wrote to Navarro Ledesma that the purpose of life could never be to raise children because all apparent goals in human life are as unattainable as the horizon which retreats as one moves toward it; «el horizonte está en los ojos y no en la realidad, y nuestro fin, que es cooperar a una obra inacabable, aunque tenga un valor real, es inapreciable y hasta digno de desprecio» (II, 1015).

Curiously, shortly after the child's birth Ganivet left for Spain. He had been granted a four-month leave and he spent from mid-December, until mid-March in Granada. Amelia and Angel Tristán apparently did not accompany him.[7]

If the birth of a child could not brighten Ganivet's cheerless vision of life, death could certainly darken it. Nine months after Ganivet had become a father for the second time his own mother died in Granada. They had been very close despite Ganivet's absence from Granada; he was, according to Herrero «el hijo predilecto de doña Angeles» (CFAG, 15), and he was much affected by this loss.

In addition to these personal troubles, Ganivet experienced considerable professional dissatisfaction while in Antwerp. Shortly after his arrival he discovered that the consulate's chief secretary was embezzling consular funds. Later, Ganivet discovered this employee to be taking official stamps and documents to his home where he performed consular services for his personal financial benefit. (In November of 1893 this employee was finally dismissed for selling false permits to shippers which allowed them to circumvent a cholera quarantine.)[8] Further, he found the consul, a Señor Serra, to be a difficult man to please, inquisitorially curious about Ganivet's affairs, and a «número uno de los percebes.» What is more, the consul's mother-in-law attempted to dictate minor consular policy, much to Ganivet's annoyance (II, 817-8). Besides these vexations, the low cultural level of his colleagues, the generally boring and routine nature of his consular duties, and the distant prospects for promotion further discouraged the young diplomat (II, 959). These factors, in addition to his unconventional union with Amelia and his distaste for hollow, prescribed behavior, help explain why, although initially he engaged in a rather active social life in diplomatic circles, he soon began to withdraw more and more, until his existence was almost solitary. He wrote to his family in the fall of 1892 that he only enjoyed himself when he was alone and free to do as he pleased (CFAG, 112). And his letter of November 17, 1893, to Navarro makes clear that his distaste for social life grew out of a refusal to fit into any of the pigeonholes in

[7] There are few recorded anecdotes about Ganivet as a father. See GALLEGO MORELL, *Angel Ganivet...*, 158-9.

[8] HERRERO, «Ganivet y su canciller en Amberes,» *Revista Hispánica Moderna*, XXX (1964), 276-8.

which society places individuals, and out of a constitutional aversion to dealing with other people:

> porque la finura de su epidermis no resiste las molestias del contacto, o porque la delicadeza de las narices no soporta el *olorcillo* que las agrupaciones humanas —como las de los demás animales— desprenden de sí. Cuando esto ocurre, no hay otro recurso que apartarse más o menos gradual y progresivamente de las expresadas agrupaciones. (I, 924)

At other times he expressed his misanthropic nature simply by refusing to conform to social conventions, which he fervently opposed and distrusted. Indeed, much of Ganivet's writing seeks to identify and praise the natural and true in individuals and societies while excoriating artificiality, often as it is manifested in material progress. The ascetic life he led in Antwerp, without artificial heat or light, was partially a result of his having declared war on all social artifices including all ceremonies, especially marriages, official receptions, and the like (II, 951), much like the life led by Pío Cid, the nonconformist protagonist of his second novel, *Los trabajos del infatigable creador, Pío Cid.*

Belgium and its culture

Ganivet's residence in Belgium coincided with a period of considerable political, economic, and cultural activity there. But in most of it Ganivet saw little to commend. His first published remarks on Belgium came just six weeks after his arrival in Antwerp in a brief polite chronicle, «Un festival literario en Amberes.» This minor piece describes the *Landjuweel,* an impressive re-enactment of the historic cortege held in Antwerp in 1561 celebrating the victory of Antwerp's literary society in a competition with societies from elsewhere in Belgium. According to Ganivet, half the population of Belgium and people from all over Europe were in attendance and he applauds the international character of the proceedings and the setting of *La Place de Meir* where he viewed the spectacle (GM: ET, 5-7).

Notwithstanding the complimentary observations, required by professional courtesy, Ganivet's views on the Belgians and their culture found quite different expression in letters to Navarro Ledesma. Indeed, he felt that if Spain somehow were to become comparable to Belgium, «mejor es curarse en salud, es decir, mejor es no curarse ni tomar medicina alguna y morir como hombres, borrarnos del mapa sin hacer nuevas contorsiones» (II, 896-7).

Ganivet continued his disparagement of the literary and artistic culture of Belgium and the Low Countries as a whole in other letters to Spain. Although he had a few words of praise for Erasmus and the Dutch poet Jacob Cats (1577-1660), he found no one of importance in recent times except the Belgian dramatist Maurice Maeterlinck, whose spiritualist essay *Le Trésor des Humbles* (1896) he particularly cherished for its delicacy (I, 981).[9] As to contemporary painting, he waved it away with words like "decadente» and «extravagante», and he deemed contemporary music beneath the name art.[10] He even maintained that the great Dutch and Flemish painters of the sixteenth and seventeenth centuries were not truly original, so influenced were they by Italians and Germans—and one of them, Rubens, was actually German born. So lacking in ardor and artistic inspiration are the Low Countries, Ganivet said, that they only produce notable art when stimulated by the example of others (II, 833).

But Ganivet did find one unequivocal treasure in Belgium's artistic heritage. This was the city of Bruges. Removed from the bustling commercialism which characterized Antwerp, Bruges was for him «la Toledo flamenca,» a city rich in eternal ideals and largely forgotten by the modern world in its rush toward progress. Bruges had flourished in the thirteenth and fourteenth centuries when it had been the major entrepôt port of the Hanseatic League, but for the vice consul the city was even greater in its decline, a decline that preserved the priceless splendour of eternal things and shunned the seductive shallow glitter of the evanescent. In the brief article, «Arte gótico,» written in November of 1895, Ganivet saw Bruges as a lesson in humility for those nations who pride themselves on their wealth and the extent of their railroad, telegraph, and telephone lines, saying these will leave behind nothing more significant than the «recuerdo... de sus prolongadas digestiones» (I, 987). By contrast, Bruges, having long since lost its commercial importance, stands as a lasting and edifying monument to the spirit that inspired gothic art, just as Granada's Alhambra exemplifies the spirit of the Arabs who dominated Spain for so long. And spiritual qualities were always more valuable to Ganivet than was material progress.[11]

Letters, life, and art

We know from his letters to friends and family a great deal about Ganivet's life in Antwerp, Helsinki and, to a lesser extent, Riga. His correspondence, one of the richest in Spanish literature, provides an important link among the author's life, character, and formal writing.[12] Ganivet's

[9] Francisco García Lorca, *Angel Ganivet y su idea del hombre* (Buenos Aires, 1952), 40, finds the influence of Maeterlinck's symbolist theatre in Ganivet's *El escultor de su alma.* Gonzalo Sobejano, «Ganivet o la soberbia,» *Cuadernos Hispanoamericanos,* 35 (1958), 138, claims that Ganivet's propensity toward the spiritual and the ethereal was fortified hy his reading of *Le Trésor des Humbles.*

[10] «Dos cartas inéditas de Angel Ganivet,» 109.

[11] Modern Belgian artists like James Enser share these views.

[12] Four volumes of Ganivet's correspondence have been published, although only one of these, a selection of letters he wrote to Francisco Navarro Ledesma, is included, under the title *Epistolario,* in his *Obras.* This volume contains thirty-one letters dated from February 18, 1893, to January 4, 1895, and represents but a small fraction of the extant correspondence between the two which stretches from June 1890 to November 18, 1898. Additional letters from Ganivet to Navarro Ledesma are published in JH, 291-331; and as «Epistolario,» in *Helios* (Madrid,

inclination to use the informal and conversational medium of letters for exploring and expressing his thoughts spills over from his correspondence itelf and becomes the format of choice for two of his key works written in Helsinki: *Granada la bella* and *Cartas finlandesas*.

Through his correspondence from Antwerp Ganivet comes alive; the letters form a kind of autobiography of emotional states, philosophical, religious, and political ruminations, patriotic concerns, and cultural and literary judgments. Further, although he had written some short pieces before his arrival in Antwerp, in the Belgian city he composed his first substantive work, and his letters chronicle his struggles with artistic creation.

Nothing marks Ganivet's correspondence from Antwerp more than recorded suffering, physical and psychological. Letter after letter records the young writer's recurring headaches, grippe, insomnia, liver and intestinal problems, skin eruptions (probably of syphilitic origin), and, most of all, depression.[13] «Contesto a tu carta bajo la impresión más penosa que puedas imaginarte,» he wrote in 1893 to Navarro Ledesma in a typical outpouring. «Aunque no me ha sucedido nada de particular no deja de ser cierto que estoy muy triste, en primer término porque lo estoy, y en segundo, porque no sé por qué lo estoy» (JA, 348).

One of Ganivet's fundamental problems, he believed, was abulia. He had already touched upon this condition in *España filosófica contemporánea* and he would elaborate on it in the *Idearium español* as it pertained to Spanish culture as a whole. In his correspondence from Antwerp he applies the idea to himself and to many of his contemporaries, including Navarro Ledesma. The abulic state, he says, is characterized by a weakening of the will and the inability to assimilate new material necessary for the vital renovation of life over time. It is immediately evident in the lack of concentration required for action. And it is most

1903), I, 265-70; II, 38-9 and 265-9; VIII, 35-45; X, 257-269; XII, 544-52; also «Epistolario,» in *Revista de Occidente,* II (1965): 273-323 and in GM: ET, 134-160. Gallego Morell indicates (88) where some other letters have been published. See JA, 339-62, for an excellent summary of the hundreds of unpublished letters now in the possession of the Hispanic Society of America in New York City. See also SEGUNDO SERRANO PONCELA, «Ganivet en sus cartas,» *Revista Hispánica Moderna,* XXIV (1958), 301-311. Unfortunately only a handful of the letters Ganivet received have been published, see GM:ET, 9-129 and *Revista de Occidente,* II (1965), 315-20. CFAG contains letters to his mother written from November 24, 1888, to August 12, 1895, and to his brother and sisters (until April 1897) after his mother's death. Almost all the letters Ganivet wrote to his family his first year in Madrid, 1888-89, have been lost. Herrero's «Introducción» to this volume is especially valuable. Another twenty-five letters written between May 25, 1895, and November 10, 1898, were published by the recipient, Nicolás María López, in *La Cofradía del Avellano* (NML). A fourth collection, *Juicio de Angel Ganivet sobre su obra literaria* (LSLP), contains eighteen letters written to Luis Seco de Lucena, the editor of *El Defensor de Granada,* and to his brother Francisco, dated from January 1896 to November 1898.

[13] JUAN V. AGUDIEZ in *Las novelas de Angel Ganivet* (New York, 1972), 27-8, argues quite convincingly that a metabolic disorder was responsible for much of the author's physical and mental distress.

prevalent in southern countries where rapidity of perception, a faulty educational system, and the madness of living in a hurry, all work to distract one's attention and dissipate concentration, thus creating, together with organic weakness, the typical aboulic personality. By contrast to this weak personality typical of the South, the personality more common in northern countries is psychologically vital. The Belgians, for example, do not suffer from abulia. They move slowly, but they are blessed with great concentration, will power, and certainty in their actions. Ganivet cites the case of a Belgian gentleman whom he had recently met, who at the age of sixty-five was beginning to learn English; Ganivet was sure that if he lived five or six more years the man would succeed.

As a remedy for abulia, Ganivet proposed a method he had used successfully himself. This was an exercise in mental associations capable of making concentration on one object possible. One must have a favorite subject of contemplation, which by virtue of its familiarity remains as a point of reference for thought in relation to other things. Turning to this subject would be something «tan práctico, como meter de nuevo en los rieles al tranvía descarrilado» (II, 815).

This remedy betrays another trait of Ganivet's mind and character: the unsatisfied need for security in knowledge and a clear purpose in life. Here the troubled man, seemingly suffering from what R. D. Laing has termed ontological insecurity, clings to a familiar idea to steady himself in a world offering no *positive* intellectual or spiritual certainty and no confident direction.[14]

These twin pains gripped Ganivet's being throughout his short adult life. By the age of twenty-five, Ganivet had come to think that he and all mankind were superflous in the world, devoid of all significant purpose: «Dígase lo que se quiera, todo requiere un fin en el mundo, y el gran desencanto llega cuando en el fin más alto se descubre el vacío» he wrote to Navarro from Antwerp (II, 1015). The only hint of purpose Ganivet discerns is the begetting of other creatures—who show no progress over their forebears—and this is merely a goal of the species, not of the individual, rendering individuals simply a part not a whole, a means and not an end. They are, Ganivet says, like motors, which seem to possess an independent existence because they function, letting off smoke or steam, but their reason for existing is merely to serve others, to whom they are chained like slaves. And in this slavery of the individual to the species, no human genius or education avails, for the least gifted and cultured men multiply more fruitfully than the artists or the wise (II, 1014; NML, 57).

The denial of truth and purpose gained such a hold over Ganivet while in Antwerp that he decided he would not trade it for the most optimistic and joyful beliefs of those who complacently live out routine lives (II, 1014). He even concluded, however fleetingly, that his clarity of vision provided the only prospect of human happiness, since for him paradise would consist of neither wanting nor believing anything. The

[14] See R. D. LAING, *The Divided Self* (New York, Pantheon, 1969), 40-3.

reputed pessimism of a believer like Thomas à Kempis struck him as ludicrous; how can one who believes be philosophically honest enough to be a pessimist? One who lives with God needs nothing further and knows nothing else. In order to be an honest and knowing pessimist, Ganivet asserts, one must believe in nothing and exist in ignorance of one's purpose in the world. «Conste que yo no creo,» he states emphatically, «ni quiero creer por ahora. Llegaré un día a encerrarme en un castillo, y a no creer ni en la existencia de los hombres» (NML, 57-8).

Ganivet dismissed the existence of God as but a fiction created by human beings, «el más humano Jesús, y lo real es que nosotros los occidentales a éste nos agregamos, por ser el último en el orden del tiempo y en el de la posibilidad» (II, 975-6). Consciously following Ludwig von Feuerbach, he proclaimed that:

> Hoy ya los dioses que nos formamos somos nosotros mismos y por esto y por no poder salir de nosotros y por encontrarnos insuficientes es por lo que nos desesperamos. Que venga la barbarie, que el hombre vuelva a embrutecerse, y no tardará en crear otros dioses... (II, 976)

Ganivet's philosophical nihilism led him to view human life fatalistically. Each one of us, he said, is moved and formed by circumstances and surroundings as if one were a piece of furniture (II, 1008) or a stone (II, 985). Whether one's actions arise spontaneously or self-consciously, they can never serve to accomplish any particular human goal, since human beings live attached to a *noria* propelled by a blindfolded mule. Sometimes we turn the wheel in vain because the well is dry; at other times we draw water unknowingly, because we cannot see what we are doing (II, 1009-10).

Ganivet uses this metaphor of the *noria* to link the idea of a purposeless existence to contempt for contemporary society. It is bad enough, he says, to plod senselessly around a dry well, but it is worse to be prevented from learning if one's efforts avail. The social system thus thwarts any possible purpose for our lives by blinding us like mules at the *noria*. "Por eso odio con toda mi alma nuestra organización y todas sus infinitas farsas, y veré con entusiasmo todos los trabajos de destrucción, aunque sea yo el primero que perezca» (II, 1010). Wanting nothing to do with this society, Ganivet says he would, if he could, make a pact with a magician to be put in an enchanted bottle and left in peace for several thousand centuries until men had grown wings, then to be resuscitated with them and live tumbling in space and eating air (II, 1010).

Seeing no prospect of reforming society and mankind, believing that humanity continues to merit a «lluvia de fuego cada mañana y un diluvio universal cada tarde» (II, 1011-2), and so wanting to escape the mindless bondage of a futile existence, Ganivet was bound to contemplate suicide. His letter of January 2, 1895, to Navarro Ledesma contains some of these utterances, and he confesses: «Pero no quiero hacer premeditadamente nada contra los deseos que yo mismo me noto muy claros y definidos, y que no pueden hacer daño a nadie más que a mí mismo...»

(II, 1012). In a letter written two days later, he again dwells on the purposelessness of existence and, in the last sentence, remarks «... puedo permitirme la satisfacción de entretenerme con mis imaginaciones para disfrazar las miserias de la vida e impedir que se acerque la idea del suicidio, que no resuelve nada tampoco...» And he adds a note of wan humor in suspecting that suicide might resolve nothing, for we might all have several editions, and as each one is used up, we are recycled and returned to life in a new one (II, 1017). Later the humor would fade as Ganivet found suicide ever more appealing and, finally, irresistible.[15]

The more of Ganivet's correspondence from Antwerp one reads the more evident it becomes that while Ganivet profoundly experienced philosophical nihilism and the general spiritual crisis of the *fin de siècle*, his intellectual and emotional miseries also arose from a sensitive temperament ill-suited to the world in which he lived and inclined to nostalgia for the socially stable, culturally rich Granada of pre-modern times and for the emotional security and religious faith he had experienced there as a child. Herrero has ascribed many of Ganivet's difficulties to his divided nature: «la paradójica unión de un espíritu de elevadísima condición moral, una mente selecta y aristocrática y una naturaleza sensual y violenta» (JH, 59). He believes, however, that Ganivet's spiritual crisis came to a head in 1895-6 when Ganivet experienced an *iluminación* which brought him «un ser y un amor nuevos» (JH, 11).

Ganivet's miseries became the more acute as a consequence of his prolonged isolation from the homeland that he both assailed and needed. To live constantly in foreign lands could only deepen his estrangement. People who frequently change their country of residence, he said, were akin to the traditional soup bone of the poor passed from pot to pot. Popular custom held that the bone's nutritional value increased by being in so many soups, but Ganivet knew the opposite was so. The same thing happens to people who move from one environment to another: «parece que van ganando porque se limpian y purifican, y hasta adquieren cierto lustre exterior; pero la sustancia creo yo que se va quedando fuera» (II, 931).

Ganivet's thoughts on this subject were rooted in a feeling that was for him more powerful than religion. He calls it the *sentimiento de la Naturaleza* and it resembles Ortega y Gasset's later conception of *circunstancia*. This feeling or sentiment draws its power from all the external elements that form an individual, that root him to his natural culture: parents, dwelling place, countryside, personal possessions, all of which contain and nourish the self. When an individual is unable to find satis-

[15] Later references to suicide are found in his letter of August 14, 1895, to Navarro, quoted in JA, 359, note 37, and NML, 73 (October, 1896). See also SERRANO PONCELA, «Ganivet en sus cartas,» 308-9. GÓMEZ MORENO, «Recuerdos de un condiscípulo,» 28, recalls that as a student at the University in Granada, «Ya entonces acariciaba el suicidio.» In «El mundo soy yo,» written while Ganivet was a student in Madrid he exclaims: «Creo en la desesperación suicida,» in JH, 284.

faction in society or the tranquility necessary for work, friendly objects of his personal and cultural past soothe the spirit. But only those which have surrounded us in our formative years, and which virtually become a part of us, possess this emotive capacity. In such an individual environment, a *yo-medio o medio-yo,* «está la tabla adonde debemos agarrarnos fuertemente antes de irnos a fondo» (II, 910, 949-50). Ganivet even imagined a kind of Noah's Ark in which he could place his cherished belongings and live forever while fleeing an evil society (II, 951).

For Ganivet, nothing made that society more evil and unendurable than the rise of Industrial Civilization. He shared this judgment with other members of the Generation of '98, most notably, Miguel de Unamuno, Azorín, and Pío Baroja, and the modernist author, Ramón del Valle Inclán. The hostility of these Spanish writers toward the increasingly machine-dominated, commercialized, utilitarian world, which they believed to be obliterating a more humane mode of existence, was also common to writers and artists elsewhere in Europe during the closing years of the 19th century.[16] Ganivet expressed his antagonism toward the new age most dramatically in *La conquista del reino de Maya* and *Granada la bella.* But his letters from Antwerp abound with flashes of this anger as well as hints of why Ganivet felt the way he did.

The principal targets of Ganivet's attack on the «época tan cochina» (II, 984) in which he lived were materialism, commercialism, mechanization, the imperfections of liberal democracy, and the senselessly rapid pace of life. Modern culture, he says, is in the grips of an artificial dynamic tendency that creates activity for its own sake and produces superficiality in everything. To what he called «el mundo locomotora» he much preferred «el mundo convento» (II, 962). He assured Navarro that "si existiera un Dios pensante... encontraría más noble y digno ese reposo chinesco de quien no se apresura por nada que esta actividad estúpida con que corremos incesantemente para no ir a ninguna parte» (II, 968). Earlier periods, although considerably less comfortable materially, produced greater creative works because they possessed more noble conceptions of life and compensated for material poverty with abundant spirituality (II, 932).

Of all the kinds of soulless activity that plague modern life none more provoked Ganivet's rage than commerce and the materialism it breeds. Money, he said, has become the one universal to which all men bow, replacing the old universals that no longer command reverence (II, 977, 998). And everywhere one looks, the eagerness for money is stripping people of their humanity and transforming them into mere money-making machines. «Estamos oprimidos por el instinto de la propiedad, y la propiedad... nos subyuga y llega a formar parte de nuestro organismo,» he says (II, 909), but few will admit it.

16 See LILY LITVAK, *A Dream of Arcadia: Anti-Industrialism in Spanish Literature,* 1895-1902 (Austin and London, 1975), for an excellent analysis of Industrial Civilization and how Unamuno, Baroja, Azorín and Valle-Inclán reacted to it. Although Ganivet is not included in this important study, he shared many of the attitudes of these authors.

Ganivet protested against this materialism in more than words. For one thing, he scarcely ate meat in Antwerp, as a way of escaping the power of money. The only truly free man, he says, in a society where men are slaves to the *peseta* and fight like animals to get it, is the man willing to nourish himself on things that cost next to nothing. «Hoy,» he writes to his family in Granada, «todos se pasan la vida suspirando por ascender en riqueza o en categoría, sin fijarse en que eso es cosa insignificante, si no se acompaña del deseo de aprovechar todos esos medios, que no son más que medios, en algo más noble» (CFAG, 185, 188). For Ganivet, the greatest advantage of not aspiring to be rich is that one can pursue the noble end of the contemplative life.

While consoling his sisters on the loss of their mother and offering counsel on their proposal to enter a convent, he confessed in the fall of 1895 his detachment from life in society and wrote that, if he had religious faith, he too might enter an order. Lacking the solace religion might provide, he chose to embrace an ascetic life within the world, with all the difficulties that might entail: «Es más fácil decidirse un día y una vez que tener que luchar mil veces cada día contra muchas imposiciones ridículas y atractivos vulgares del mundo...» (CFAG, 257). In November he explained to Nicolás María López that he had broken with society and was living only within four walls: «Acaso sea... preferible, bien que en el fondo sea también un suicidio lento pero continuo» (NML, 55).

Ganivet discerned and belabored several evil consequences for society of the reigning commercialism and materialism. He finds it quite natural that, amidst the furor for money, the laborers who spend their lives working for the same miserable wages feel rage against society. Ganivet noted the unrest among the working classes in Spain and Belgium, the growing socialist movement, and the anarchist violence of the 1890's as the first sparks of serious problems. Horrified at the sight of a weaver in the British pavilion of the Antwerp International Exposition who worked at his loom as if he were a part of it, Ganivet complained that such «hombres máquina» must be dehumanized imbeciles or, should they ever reflect on their condition, become nihilists. Human beings and society must pay a price either way for this oppression by a despot «peor que cien Nerones juntos» (II, 978).

Closely related to the dehumanization of people through money and machines was the degrading uniformity that threatened to sweep across modern culture.[17] Decrying the herd instinct then asserting itself through the ascendency of the lower classes, Ganivet declared that it was high time for everyone to rebel against the «pecuarismo» that makes social life impossible. Culture thrives on difference not sameness, he said: «preferible es la variedad atómica a la uniformidad asnal» (II, 945).

Nowhere did Ganivet find this «pecuarismo» more evident and perilous than in politics. Democracy, with its ever expanding franchise, would only debase politics and bring the unruly and uneducated masses to

[17] Gustavo Adolfo Bécquer had made similar observations in the 1860's.

power. Agreeing with Ibsen's assertion in *An Enemy of the People* that «estando compuesta de imbéciles la mayoría, la minoría es la que debe gobernar» (II, 927), Ganivet feared that democracy had given the masses an exaggerated sense of self-importance. People, Ganivet believed, must know their place; neither the accumulation of wealth nor the superficial aping of dress, style or manners would be sufficient to elevate a person into a higher class. For commoners to rise socially, they would have to make a profound, individual effort at a «depuración de la materia bruta» (II, 983). The process most assuredly could not be accomplished by obtaining the right to vote.

Ganivet claims to have had no antagonism toward the lower class. He merely judged it to be naturally «baja y ruin,» like the manure used to fertilize the fields: it is appropriate in its place. As he remarked in a letter, a piece of cattle dung is not annoying in the middle of a path, nor in a field, nor in a dung heap, because these are natural places for it, and it can even be quite useful. But, if you put the same piece of dung under a bell jar as a centerpiece, it is unbearable (II, 982). Thus the role of the masses is not to lead, but to follow. Who ever heard of a muleteer consulting with his donkeys when the donkeys' job is simply to carry the load? This is how Ganivet saw the proponents of democracy, and he was certain that the end result will be disastrous.

Ganivet condemned any theory of history born of the adulation of the masses, and which credits the common folk with every historical change. Such theoretical constructs falsify history, he says, as the example of Napoleon clearly demonstrates. Napoleon was not merely a man who expressed the will and aspirations of the people. Amidst a nation in chaos he alone was able to suppress competing factions and form a stable government, create twenty armies, and conquer half of Europe. It is sheer foolishness, Ganivet asserted, to diminish Napoleon's role as an individual by interpreting his actions as the «adivinación de las masas» (II, 929).

Ganivet also took Napoleon as a model ruler. Viewing his people as herds of sheep, the French dictator treated them like a good shepherd, with beatings when necessary (II, 886). Like Napoleon, Ganivet said, a competent ruler must make himself respected and feared. He must possess great passions without falling prey to commonplace prejudices. A ruler with too high an opinion of his subjects reveals his own weakness; a strong leader will feel repugnance and disgust for ordinary people and things. His creed must affirm «mucho amor y mucho palo para los pequeños, y mucho desprecio y mucha autoridad para los grandes» (II, 892).

A conservative who prized order, authority, and excellence, Ganivet lamented on several occasions the absence of a leader strong enough to set things in order, even though that would require forceful, even violent, methods. Ganivet saw «la inmunda democracia» undermining all culture by promising power to those who had always been excluded and by obliging politicians to court the general populace with vulgar and impossible promises of happiness and prosperity. This can only lead to greed and sloth and weakness since government cannot provide happiness to the governed: «Hay que aguantarse con lo que venga porque el mundo está constituido así y no pensar en Jaujas imposibles» (II, 887).

Ganivet's own political motto was «Patria, paciencia y trabajar» and his criticism of democracy was basically a patriotic one. Living abroad had made the young diplomat more aware of Spain's strengths (and weaknesses) and sharpened his concern with her future. He was hungry for news of his «querida patria, que ahora empiezo a comprender y a amar» (JA, 354). If the patriotic furor aroused over national setbacks could last, he thought, maybe people would accustom themselves to paying their taxes more regularly. Sentiments he would repeat in the *Idearium* are expressed in a letter home to Granada in November of 1893: «El patriotismo debería consistir en trabajar calladamente hasta que fuésemos una nación formal y capaz de imponer respeto a los que hoy por hoy nos paran cuando quieren con un pedazo de papel» (CFAG, 166). But strong as were Ganivet's feelings about his homeland, they were not so much political as a reflection of a nostalgia for the Granada of his youth. For him, *patria* meant the environment that one had assimilated during the formative years of childhood and youth and that shaped almost all of one's psychological being (II, 910). Indeed, Ganivet's very conception of a desirable political community, as set forth in his Antwerp correspondence, seems drawn from his idealization of provincial Granada. He dreamed of transforming his home town into an artistic and cultural center along the lines of the Greek city states and the cities of the Italian Renaissance which he admired enormously.

What made the Greek and Italian models so appealing to Ganivet was the artistic environment made possible by the absence of stifling ties of political union. These city-states were clearly free from what the author judged the most profound political error of his times: the desire to unify and centralize into great nation states. Ganivet held this desire largely responsible for the calamitous times in which he lived. For the great nations, such as Germany, supposedly embodying an advanced political form, were to him really artificial constructs that had severely limited the natural life and spirit of the more vital, smaller states from which they grew. Ganivet particularly lamented the nation-state's monotonous uniformity, and in the case of Germany, he feared the seduction exercised by military values over the national mind.[18]

In Spain the process of centralization had worked to the lasting detriment of cultural vitality. Forty or fifty years earlier, Ganivet said, there were numerous independent, provincial intellectual circles which produced important cultural figures throughout the country. In Granada, for example, such notables as Pedro Antonio Alarcón and Juan Valera had fed on local traditions.[19] But nationalism had destroyed this diverse, provincial, cultural richness. Nowadays, Ganivet complained, young men

[18] See «Angel Ganivet: Epistolario,» *Helios* V (1903), 260-5, letter of February 19, 1894.

[19] See ANTONIO GALLEGO MORELL, *Angel Ganivet...*, 25-32, for a brief background of Granada's intellectual life in the period Ganivet spent there.

(like himself), disgusted by arid local life, flock to Madrid as soon as they finish their studies, there to lead artistically unproductive, anonymous lives. The metropolis almost always destroys new talent, he said, for it is overnourished by constant stimuli, and at the same time is psychologically dissipated. Writers and artists work best in their native environment, where they can create naturally. But when national centers attract and consume all creative energies, only artifice, extravagance, decadence, and overall impoverishment of cultural life can result (II, 965-8).[20]

Certainly, artists who understand life in Madrid, like Galdós, should live and produce their works there. But those who do not, or who cannot adjust to life in the capital, or who could make valuable contributions to their local culture, such as Emilia Pardo Bazán and José María de Pereda, should stay home. Their work can maintain and revitalize local culture and thereby raise the cultural level of the nation as a whole. But to try to elevate cultural life through centralization is to achieve spurious not substantive success.

Ganivet thus urged upon his friends the reorganization of every city as a semi-autonomous *polis,* where the citizens could live as a family, strolling about in their shirt sleeves and perhaps even philosophizing under the direction of an Aristotle. If this could be achieved, a practical variety of socialism could then be easily realized: the soup kitchen designed for those who are either unwilling or unable to work and are satisfied by having their alimentary needs met, and for those who have nobler things to do than to win bread. Ganivet was convinced that a nation where everyone is assured of eating every day would be the most tranquil and productive. There would be idlers, it is true, but there would be no terrorists; there would be those who live without thinking, but there would also be those who spend all their time thinking, untroubled by petty concerns. «Este socialismo anárquico—nirvánico es el mío,» he says. "Este es mi credo filosófico—político, económico, familiar y religioso» (II, 968). Ganivet acknowledged that these ideas would not find favor with the commercial and industrial classes, «pero es lo humano y aun lo divino...»

Although Ganivet's political creed was communicated as a highly personal statement to a close friend and should not be judged as a final product of the author's thought, it does share a number of characteristics with writings he intended for publication. For one thing, it betrays Ganivet's naïveté about economic and legal realities. Ganivet makes no provision, for instance, for the production of the goods needed to supply the food to be distributed to all, nor does he provide any system of authority. Possibly, as a legacy of his distaste for the legal profession and bureaucracy and of his ingenuous attribution of coercive power to the teaching profession in *España filosófica contemporánea,* he hoped ideas would exercise a force of their own. But if in its naïveté this sketchily drawn utopia is deficient as a model for human society, it

[20] *Los trabajos* (II, 367) offers a similar yet more desolate view of urban life.

does give expression to the author's most cherished ideals: contemplation, tranquility, and intellectual discourse among peers and the precedence of spiritual over material values.

Withdrawal from a large, complex, competitive, commercial, materialistic, centralized, hierarchical society is a constant aspiration of Ganivet's writing. To Ganivet's despair it was a withdrawal he was never completely able to achieve, except in literary form and suicide. Significantly, images of retreat and withdrawal appear frequently in both his private correspondence and his work intended for publication—and his very last literary image, in *El escultor de su alma,* describes the artist Pedro Mártir's death in a cave, a retreat from the world.

Ganivet's views on writing and literature

While in Belgium, Ganivet began to think of himself as a writer, and he found the prospects for writers of quality very bleak in his homeland due to commercialism and the «estupidez colectiva» of the majority (II, 933). If only Spain had patrons of the arts, he mused, then writers might be able to rise above vulgarity. But those with sufficient capital to invest were also captives of commerce and thus willing to participate only in ventures certain to turn a quick profit. «¿Qué arte,» he asks, «puede prosperar en una sociedad que aplaude el discurso borrical de Torquemada...?» (NML, 55).

Ganivet also discussed in his letters to Navarro a variety of factors directly related to the composition of literary works. He was strongly opposed to «novelas de tesis» which he found lacking both in interest and more importantly in «la pureza que los asuntos artísticos deben tener» (II, 879). He held that an artist must not merely take his impressions from reality but these impressions must be subjected to a personal vision, not merely transcribed in the heat of the moment. «Para componer se necesita estar lleno de impresiones, pero éstas no dicen nada mientras no las fecunda esa idea constante de que yo te hablaba. Por esto, los que escriben excitados por la pasión caen en el sentimentalismo y en la hinchazón» (II, 850). A poet should have an «idea constante... Sea cual fuere el matiz, será bueno si se refleja constantemente» in his work.

The principal art of a poet, he commented to Navarro in July of 1893, is in knowing that the reader likes to see:

> como en un hecho que a él nada le decía el artista encuentra bellezas ocultas, y que, descubiertas, parece imposible que no haya podido descubrirlas todo el mundo de puro naturales y sencillas, y hasta vulgares. Los inventores son los que «caen» en cosas en que los demás no habíamos «caído,» y a los poetas les pasa lo propio; por esto al poeta se le conceden todas las libertades menos una: la de adulterar la realidad, sacando de ella consecuencias impropias, violentas o forzadas. (II, 875)

The artist then sees that which exists in reality and is true but has escaped the notice of the ordinary individual. Indeed, this closely approximates the credo of Pío Cid in *Los trabajos del infatigable creador, Pío Cid* who discovers hidden virtues in the souls of the simple and the grand.

Ganivet rejects classicism and its bare «skeletons» in favor of an aesthetic which is more inclusive of life in a given moment: «Compárese cualquier *Dúo* o cualquier *Partida de juego* de los pintores meridionales con el *Dúo* y la *Partida* de Teniers,» he tells Navarro. «En los primeros, personas, expresión; en el segundo, personas, expresión, mesas, sillas, cazuelas, gato, candil, botijos, etc. ... Tú tienes simpatía por este segundo modo de ver las cosas, y yo te aplaudo, porque es el mío...» (II, 871). *La conquista,* which Ganivet was working on at the time he made this comment to Navarro, clearly reflects its author's desire to portray the «mesas, sillas, cazuelas, ...» etc., of life in Maya with the eye of a *costumbrista.*

Not long after this, on July 24, 1893, Ganivet tells Navarro that he does not want to show him his work in progress because he is afraid that Navarro's unfavorable opinion would be terribly discouraging and he then might not finish the work. He goes on to compare a work of art to an «hijo,» which a parent must love and care for, even if it is born with a defect. The image is noteworthy since, five years later in his play *El escultor de su alma,* the artist's masterpiece is Alma, his own daughter.

In addition to commenting on his own developing aesthetic ideas, Ganivet frequently exchanged opinions with his correspondents on Spanish and foreign literature, and these references, although random, help chart his literary concerns and provide clues to the masters who may have influenced his own work.[21]

Cervantes was probably the author Ganivet most admired; early in *La conquista,* which he began in Antwerp in the spring of 1893, he pays homage to him, and there are many references to the man and his supreme work, *Don Quixote.* He also admired Francisco de Quevedo, whose biting satire may have influenced *La conquista,* and Lope de Vega whose works he found difficult to appreciate off the stage (II, 923, 825; LSLP, 31). Mateo Alemán's *Guzmán de Alfarache* and Swift's *Gulliver's Travels* he cites as examples of works he has been unable to finish because they are, like many truly great works, «pesadas y fatigosas.»[22] He praises the «dos sublimes histéricos,» Santa Teresa and San Juan de la Cruz (II, 1011), as well as Fray Luis de León for whom he had a spiritual affinity based on León's conception of the ideal «Vida retirada» close to nature. He highly recommended Fray Luis of Granada's *Libro de la oración y meditación* to Navarro Ledesma as a «manual de oro macizo» (II, 815).[23]

The contemporary novelist he most admired was Benito Pérez Galdós, whose work he followed with great interest. He was distressed that

[21] See William Harris Shuford, «Angel Ganivet as a Literary Critic,» unpublished doctoral dissertation, University of North Carolina, Chapel Hill, 1964, for a comprehensive discussion of Ganivet's references to other authors.

[22] «Epistolario,» *Revista de Occidente,* II (1965), 307.

[23] JH, 196, suggests Fray Luis de Granada's influence on Ganivet.

Galdós was virtually unknown abroad.[24] He remarked sadly to Navarro Ledesma that only two people in all Antwerp had ever heard of the great Spanish author: the former secretary of the consulate, who believed him to be an elementary education inspector, and the consul, who referred to him as Pedro Galdo (II, 960).

Ganivet had not always so esteemed his great contemporary. In 1889, in *España filosófica contemporánea,* he had noted with dismay a skeptical bent in Galdós (II, 614), but by 1894 his opinion had changed because Galdós had changed, and Ganivet wrote to Navarro Ledesma that it was rare for an author to begin writing with «glacial skepticism» and to move from there to a youthful idealism, as Galdós had done. Ganivet now found Galdós' works progressively warmer and more humorous and he used those works to develop his own criteria for judging the novel (II, 990). He praises *Torquemada en purgatorio* (1894), for example, on two counts: its accurate reflection of the inhuman, commercial values of contemporary society, together with the destructive atmosphere they produce, and its consummate artistic unity (II, 954) (CFAG, 203), so superior to Molière's static and lifeless version of the same person (II, 953).

Ganivet was much less complimentary of Galdós' dramas than of his novels. He deemed Galdós' dramatic situations too logical, the plot developments too methodical and novelistic, and the characterizations dependent on narrative rather than dramatic devices. Given Galdós' flaws as a dramatist, Ganivet believed the novelist should stick to novels. For even though Galdós could write acceptable, even interesting, plays, Ganivet thought it a crime that someone who could be a Mozart should waste his time being a merely adequate painter (II, 973-4).

Another contemporary Spanish novelist whom Ganivet admired was Pedro Antonio de Alarcón, a native son of Granada whom he considered a magnificent stylist whose use of local color greatly enhanced his works without depriving them of national and even universal interest. He notes that Alarcón wrote as if he were a believer when he was actually a skeptic (I, 107 and II, 1003), but this more positive viewpoint, Ganivet held, was beneficial to Alarcón's art.

Ganivet's correspondence contains but few references to poets of the day. The one who elicits praise and reflections on the art of poetry is the now obscure Federico Balart, whose elegiac work *Dolores,* written in memory of his dead wife, the young diplomat admired. The qualities Ganivet praises in this work are those attractive to his own melancholic and withdrawn temperament. Thus he finds the force of these poems in the solitude that surrounds the author. Although recognizing that the sentiment of lost love is a very common one, Ganivet notes that it can be moving when the sufferer experiences its effects in a poetic frame

[24] See RICHARD RICARD, «Deux Romanciers, Ganivet et Galdós: Affinités et Oppositions,» *Bulletin Hispanique,* LX, No. 4 (October-December 1958), 484-499, and JUAN V. AGUDIEZ, «Ganivet en las huellas de Galdós y Alarcón,» *Nueva Revista de Filología Hispánica,* vol. 16 (1962), 89-95. Ganivet also comments on the stylistic similarities between Galdós and Cervantes (II, 990).

of mind, removing himself from all practical concerns in order to live with his memories and his pain (II, 956-9).[25]

Most of Ganivet's remarks on foreign literature in the correspondence focus on French letters. Like many Spaniards and other Europeans, Ganivet was not pleased by the reputation of cultural superiority enjoyed by France and especially the French language. He asserts that French artists and intellectuals are in no way superior to the Spanish, they merely «traducir, imitar y estropear lo que otras naciones crean» in a language having the advantage of being read by cultured persons all over the world (NML, 53). Ganivet cites as an example of the misplaced status of the French the total neglect elsewhere in Europe of the well-known Spanish author José María Pereda by contrast to the great celebrity of that minor French talent, Pierre Loti. Ganivet insists that Pereda far surpasses Loti as a writer and student of human nature because he understands and conveys sentiment, not just intellect. Ganivet even claims that vast popularity cheapens French culture, for when works of art, like women, belong to many they really belong to no one (II, 934-5).

Besides his polemical jabs at the hegemony of French culture, Ganivet makes frequent and usually disparaging remarks about major French literary and intellectual figures of past and present. He had little use for the authors of the classical period, whose characters struck him as mere essences lacking all humanity, vitality, and sensuality, and whose artistry he thought beautiful only in the way a marble statute is beautiful: formal and lifeless. It was to clothe these classical skeletons with flesh, he said, that the romantic and realist movements had arisen. And upon sending his friend Nicolás María López two volumes of the works of the great classicist, Jean Racine, he recommended the plays for their serene and beautiful if artificial poetry but said that, aside from their formal qualities, all the rest of Racine is nonsense. Ganivet would not grant Molière even this grudging praise. Molière, he said, was a mere imitator who could not free himself from used patterns (II, 945) picked up from authors like Plautus (as in *L'Avare,* 1668) and Lope (as in *Le Dépit Amoureux,* 1656) (II, 943). And lack of originality was one artistic offense Ganivet did not easily forgive.

Much as Ganivet disapproved of the seventeenth-century classicists, the great French authors of the 18th Century Enlightenment—eg., Voltaire, Rousseau, Diderot—seem to have interested him not at all, for he makes no substantive reference to them.

With the French writers of the 19th century it is quite different. Most of them receive at least passing notice, and a number provoked Ganivet's strong response, clearly registering his tastes, temperament, and philosophy. Victor Hugo and Honoré de Balzac are hailed as geniuses. Their writings were after all at once idealistic and close to the pulse of life that Ganivet believed so essential to great literature. But Ganivet

[25] Ganivet also read a series of articles by Balart entitled «Algo más cerca del suicidio,» GALLEGO MORELL, *Angel Ganivet...*, 92.

dismissed all the work of the Naturalists Zola and the Goncourt Brothers and almost all of Flaubert, as «una guasa fúnebre» because it takes itself so seriously (II, 991). Although this remark is practically the only reference to Flaubert and the Goncourts in Ganivet's works, Zola's name appears often.

It is clear that Ganivet read a number of Zola's works, including at least part of the 1894 trilogy *Les Trois Villes,* to which he devoted a critical essay. Ganivet seems to have taken Zola as the leading contemporary exemplar of much that he despised in modern literature. Upon reading a fragment of *Lourdes* in a newspaper, for example, he was prompted to report to a friend his distaste for Zola's technique. He calls Zola's detailed description of a train of sick people going to the shrine a piece of foolishness, and snaps that «sólo a un necio ensoberbecido se le ocurre meter el 'escalpelo del análisis' en un cuadro humano cuya composición es tan puramente sentimental» (II, 991). Under serious consideration, the scene evaporates, leaving only the remains of hopeless creatures, repugnant in their stupidity and ill-fortune. Zola, says Ganivet, is a writer who deceives the unwary reader. He does not merely use literary techniques, he exploits them. Like a swimmer who chooses to go against the current, he impresses with dramatic effects. But eventually he tires and cannot continue, accomplishing nothing. The time will come, says Ganivet, when Zola's deceptions will be recognized and his reputation collapse taking with it foolish admirers like Clarín (II, 991-3).

Ganivet's reactions to contemporary French writers were not confined to masters of fiction. Ganivet also steeped himself in criticism. Before leaving Madrid, he had begun reading Sainte-Beuve's *Causeries du lundi,* and his few comments on this work chide the author for thinking on a high plane but expressing judgments born of ordinary existence rather than of careful thought (II, 869). More than Sainte-Beuve, Ernest Renan and Hippolyte Taine engaged Ganivet's mind and provoked his judgment. Ganivet read both Renan's *Histoire du peuple d'Israël* and his eight-volume *Les Origines du Christianisme,* with its controversial *Vie de Jésus* (1863), which Ganivet considered the weakest part because it mixed sentimental themes appropriate to the pulpit with the historical criticism. But the principal defect of *Les Origines du Christianisme* lay for Ganivet in the incompleteness of its criticism. Either Renan cannot, or he refuses to, break completely with the claims of religion. The result is that, when Renan «falls asleep» the work is not, as it purports to be, a critical rationalist history of religion but a rationalistic explanation of theological themes and dogma. Ganivet tells Navarro Ledesma that students of religion should limit themselves to purely historical sources, even at the cost of incomplete results, rather than to interpret ecclesiastical sources rationally, since this produces the same superficial effect as covering a statue with human skin to give it greater artistic value.

The *granadino* claims to be more profoundly radical than the Frenchman, because he denies all ecclesiastical assertions and practical precepts of religion while accepting the idealistic vision, which he refuses to diminish with critical swipes. One can desire a Venus more perfect than the classic one, without being a pagan, he says, and one can long for a Christ more divine than the one of tradition without being a Christian. It was noble idealism that created and sustained these deities; it is vulgar human vanity to wish to destroy them. The critics may be incensed by the ignorance that blinds people to the truth, but, says Ganivet, foreshadowing Unamuno's anguished priest San Manuel Bueno, «si no hubiera ignorancia y nos quedáramos todos con la verdad solo, ¡valiente *juerga* nos esperaba!» (II, 826).

Ganivet held Hippolyte Taine in much higher esteem than Renan, although Taine's methods were similar to those of the Naturalists whom Ganivet despised (II, 829). Renan seemed to Ganivet to be a century behind Taine. Oddly, Ganivet thought Taine was *English* (and not just a historian of English literature) and he attributed the marked difference in temperament between these two authors to their different nationalities.[26] Renan, being French, Ganivet says, is burdened with prejudices, pretensions, and arrogance, like all Frenchmen. By contrast, he found Taine more perceptive, possessed of more common sense and inclined toward an English methodicalness, cold, hard, compact, and even tiresome. It is probable that Ganivet's admiration for Taine as a student of literature and national temperament went deep enough to affect his perceptions of his own homeland. For as Herbert Ramsden has convincingly demonstrated, *Idearium español* utilizes some of the same interpretative schemes as Taine's *Histoire de la littérature anglaise,* most notably the notion that geography helps determine a nation's character.[27]

Taine may have been the only Frenchman to stimulate and contribute to Ganivet's ideas of literature, but he was not the only foreign author to do so. It is no coincidence that Ganivet admired Taine *as an Englishman,* for Ganivet respected the English, and particularly Shakespeare, and learned from them more than from any other non-Spanish writers.[28] Most of his references to Shakespeare appear in his correspondence with Navarro Ledesma, where Ganivet elaborates a theory of the sublime and the ridiculous in art. He developed this theory partially in response to an essay by Jean Psichari laboring the commonplace that only a thin line separates the sublime from the ridiculous and that only an artist brave enough to create profoundly ridiculous characters creates enduring ones (II, 844-7). Ganivet's own ideas on this theme revolve around the image of the madman as the perfect subject of art. For the madman unites mirth and pathos, illusion and reality, nonsense and wisdom, just as writers do.

In another letter Ganivet refines his terms. Taking a suggestion from Navarro Ledesma, he identifies the «Ridiculous» with the *hombre exterior*

[26] SHUFFORD, «Angel Ganivet...,» 246, suggests that the difficulty of obtaining foreign-language books in Antwerp may have led Ganivet to believe that Taine's *Histoire de la littérature anglaise* was a French translation of an English work.

[27] *Angel Ganivet's 'Idearium español': A Critical Study, passim.*

[28] Ganivet read some English works in Spanish, French, and German translations, although, probably starting in 1895, he began reading them in the original.

and «Madness» with the *hombre interior*. The exterior man (and this is an aspect of everyone) is ridiculous by being ordinary. An ordinary, prosaically ridiculous, *exterior* man best serves an artist by standing in contrast to the more complicated interior man. The *hombre interior* (and rare they are) is the madman whom common people call *chiflado*, anthropologists *vesánico*, and artists *apasionado*. According to Ganivet a truly artistically formed character is one combining in a natural way the traits of both types of men. He will be both ridiculous and deep, amusing and sorrowful (II, 867-9).

Ganivet takes Shakespeare's Falstaff, in *Henry IV* and *The Merry Wives of Windsor*, to be an excellent example of what he describes: a character who is ridiculous but also serious and profound because he mingles public buffoonery with private passion, inspiring tenderness. His *exterior* may be ridiculous, but when we see him returning time after time from his amorous appointments thwarted but laughing, we understand that there is something sublime in the *interior* of this man that makes him capable of enduring one affront after another. Ganivet calls this quality madness, although he acknowledges that other words could also be used. He argues that this madness exalts the ridiculous, making it noble rather than just laughable. Thus the hunchback who futilely seeks love is as sublime as the man who futilely seeks heaven; both are ridiculous through their profound, irrational passion. For this reason, Ganivet declares Falstaff (and Othello and Hamlet as well) to be as sublime as Prometheus.[29] His own character, Adolfo de la Gandaria, in *Los trabajos del infatigable creador, Pío Cid*, hovers between the sublime and the ridiculous in the third chapter of the novel. Rejected by a woman who loves another, he seems ridiculous, yet able when, to overcome his rejection and write a poem about it, he approaches the sublime (II, 260).

In addition to Shakespeare, other English authors Ganivet admired were Shelley, Dryden, Pope, and Milton; Dickens, Swift, Sterne, Carlyle, and Macaulay. In 1895, Ganivet signalled a newfound admiration for Jonathan Swift by sending Nicolás María López a two-volume French edition of Swift's *Gulliver's Travels* with the recommendation that this novel was the perfect example of satirical humor. Nothing had ever been written, he said, with such bitter intentions as this work by a man driven mad by hatred of mankind. And he repeated Taine's compliment crediting the raging Swift with proving that a palace is also beautiful when it burns —and perhaps even more beautiful (NML, 47).

Ganivet found Laurence Sterne's humor to be more English and more human than Swift's and he labeled him a precursor of the modern psychological writers from Taine to Paul Bourget. In September of 1895, Ganivet sent his friend López a Spanish translation of *Tristram Shandy*,

[29] LIONEL TRILLING, *The Opposing Self* (London, 1955), 38-9, gives a similar interpretation of Shakespeare's genius. Not only Shakespeare, but Ibsen, Tolstoy, and even, curiously, Zola have, for Ganivet, the ability to portray man's folly seriously by first presenting the ridiculous traits, and then exposing the mental disorder at just the right moment as to cut off our laughter.

commending its modernity and offering meditations on it that prefigure the aesthetics of his own novel *Los trabajos del infatigable creador, Pío Cid.*[30] He praised Sterne in particular for exploring the interior of a character and making fictional human beings seem more human than living beings, who are only visible within the constraints of a superficial and distorting society, and for not writing melodramatic plots (NML, 51).

In his role as literary advisor to López, Ganivet also urged his friend to round out his knowledge of the English humorists by reading a Spanish translation of Thomas Carlyle's *Heroes and Hero Worship.* The *granadino* thought Carlyle a great philosophical humorist and he shared his preachments about work, duty, and renunciation.

Another nineteenth-century English essayist whom Ganivet admired, but with whom he also took issue, was Thomas Macaulay. In his correspondence with Navarro, Ganivet rails against those who blame Catholicism for the decay of predominantly Catholic countries and credit Protestantism for the progress of others. And he expresses disappointment that Macaulay, whose independent spirit had so impressed him, supports this view. This lapse on Macaulay's part demonstrated to Ganivet that even a highly energetic mind can fall into the trap of accepting commonplaces in order to avoid the bother of penetrating further into an issue (II, 858).

By contrast to the many comments on French and English writers in his letters, Ganivet rarely mentions German writers or their works, although he was probably much influenced by a few Germans to whom he refers either superficially or not at all. Schopenhauer and Nietzsche, in particular, have been cited by critics as influential figures in Ganivet's work and, although Ganivet never mentions Nietzsche and seldom mentions Schopenhauer in his correspondence, some of the similarities between their ideas and his are striking. He remarked that the pessimistic conclusions of Zola's *Le Docteur Pascal* had already been philosophically advanced by Schopenhauer in his *Metaphysics of Love,* in which he affirms that men are miserable servants of the species and their servitude merely provides them with deceptive and brutal pleasure (II, 849). Although Nietzsche's name does not appear in Ganivet's published correspondence, Ganivet's acquaintance with Nietzsche is attested by a reference in the *Cartas finlandesas* to the brilliant paradoxes of the German philosopher then currently in vogue (I, 762-3). Gonzalo Sobejano, after a careful examination of Ganivet's works concludes: «Aunque no hayamos demostrado la relación efectiva de Ganivet a Nietzsche, relación indemostrable a nuestro juicio, tras estas comparaciones quedará acaso más claro que hasta la fecha el vínculo entre el pensamiento de ambos, debido más bien a coincidencia que a influjo.»[31]

Ganivet's correspondence contains references to a number of other important German writers, notably Johann Wolfgang von Goethe, Fried-

[30] Discussed in Chapter 5 of this study. Ganivet also sent López a translation of Sterne's *A Sentimental Journey Through France and Italy,* which he advised him to read carefully, particularly between the lines.

[31] *Nietzsche en España* (Madrid, 1967), 276.

rich Schiller, and Heinrich Heine, indicating at least a familiarity with them.[32] And the Spaniard was plainly fascinated by the differences between German and French literature. After reading an unnamed comparative study of the novels of these two nations, Ganivet said he was sure that if a resident of the moon were to read those novels he would have a perfect understanding of both countries. For everything German in the nineteenth century was massive, stolid, full of ideas and even metaphysics, whereas everything French was almost flighty, lacking in durability, and exaggerated with nothing to teach. Ganivet later expanded upon these perceptions of literature as a reflection of national character in *Idearium español.*

From Ganivet's Antwerp correspondence it is clear that he gave considerable thought to issues of artistic creation in general and literary aesthetics in particular and ideas he espoused here, such as his preference for psychological over melodramatic fiction, and his preoccupation with spiritual values and national character, provided the very substance of his books, just as his oft-spoken loneliness and suicidal despair marked the temper of his life.

«*La conquista de Maya*»

Belgium's colonial expansion during the reign of Leopold II elicited much interest and criticism from Ganivet, who, not surprisingly, viewed the whole operation as «una empresa comercial en grande, encubierta con rótulos filantrópicos» (II, 820). The venture began in 1878 when Leopold II commissioned the British explorer Henry Morton Stanley, «inculto y cruel» and insensitive to what he saw on the African continent (II, 855), according to Ganivet, to explore further and to conclude treaties on the King's behalf with local rulers. In 1885 Leopold organized the Congo Free State with himself as absolute monarch and chief stockholder in the company formed to exploit the region's resources.[33]

In the spring of 1893 Ganivet acquired a personal connection with Belgium's colonial adventure through his brief acquaintance with Agatón Tinoco, a Nicaraguan then dying in an Antwerp hospital of yellow fever contracted in the Congo and whom Ganivet as Spanish vice consul had been called to comfort. He found Tinoco to be an «obscure hero,» of great strength of purpose, integrity, humility, and devotion to causes greater than himself, unlike the many so-called «héroes» who returned from Africa to bask in public glory (I, 253-5; II, 819-20). Ganivet saw

[32] JH, 197-203, discusses the influence of German Romanticism on Ganivet.
[33] By 1904, reports of abuses against the native workers in mines and on rubber plantations provoked international protest. Leopold ceded to Belgium his interest in the Free State and in 1908 it became the colony of the Belgian Congo. SELWEN JAMES, *South of the Congo* (New York, 1943), 305, commented: «There was only one man who could be accused of the outrages which reduced the native population [of the Congo] from between 20 to 40 million in 1890 to 8,500,000 in 1911—Leopold II.»

no true heroism in men who put on airs of having contributed to a noble mission when they were merely agents of exploitation in the King's business venture. «Cualquiera que piense,» Ganivet wrote to Navarro,

> comprende que no se trata de la felicidad de la raza negra, ni del progreso, ni de nada por el estilo... Lo que suelen hacer hoy los europeos en muchos puntos de Africa, es destruir la obra de los árabes, los únicos que, aunque sea empleando la esclavitud, tienen condiciones para mejorar esos pueblos retrasados. (II, 821)

It should be added that while the Belgians were so proudly hailing their colonial heroes, and France, Germany, and England were also ruthlessly staking out territories in Africa, Ganivet had hopes that Spain would extend herself into that continent, too, and yet bring genuine civilization not ravenous exploitation. But that was not to be. For Spain was experiencing an irreversible decline in its colonial fortunes, evidenced by the movement of Spanish troops into North Africa in a futile attempt to bolster Spain's sagging prestige and strengthen its hold on Ceuta and Melilla. The situation in Cuba, destined to have a dramatic climax, was also continually deteriorating.

Ganivet probably began writing his novel *La conquista del reino de Maya por el último conquistador español, Pío Cid,* in the late spring of 1893, almost a year after arriving in Antwerp. He appears to have worked on it steadily and enthusiastically from the beginning, often writing at night and correcting and copying the manuscript during the day at his office—a practice that may have contributed to the friction he complained of there.[34] A summer cholera epidemic then reduced the flow of sea traffic in and out of Antwerp, thus giving Ganivet more time for his writing; and by mid-August he had 17 chapters written with another six projected to complete the manuscript (II, 882). Toward the end of September and again in October he reaffirmed his desire to finish the work rapidly, despite the non-literary concerns that burdened him (CFAG, 162; II, 912). Then, oddly enough, he did not mention the book again in his correspondence for almost two years.

Not until October 11, 1895, in a letter to his brother and sisters, did the novel reappear, when Ganivet said he might finish it that very night (CFAG, 256). But six weeks later, on November 23, he wrote to Navarro Ledesma that the work was still not completed. He also told his friend that a recent rereading of the 300 pages written more than two years earlier had left him thinking it worthy of burning—albeit better than his other writings.[35] Nonetheless, he vowed to add a chapter of some 40 or 50 sheets as a conclusion to this book that he called a

[34] See AGUDIEZ, *Las novelas...*, 54. This friction found literary expression in the final pages of the novel in which Pío Cid, employed in the Spanish bureaucracy, complains that his unworthy superiors reprimand him for tardiness and for writing his memoirs in his spare time while his colleagues spend these moments discussing topics about which they know nothing (I, 647).

[35] AGUDIEZ, *Las novelas...*, 55-6.

«recuerdo de mi salvajismo y brutalidad.»[36] Finally, on December 20, 1895, he could inform his family in Granada that the novel was finished (CFAG, 262).[37]

There are more references to *La conquista* in Ganivet's correspondence than to any of his other works. During the book's composition (except for the two year hiatus) and after, the author remarked on the difficulties and satisfactions of writing and asserted the novel's originality and unique position in Spanish literature. He described it as something he had to get out of his system, like a roadblock he needed to remove before he could proceed to other more important endeavors. He also compared himself to a rat pregnant with an elephant, so great did he believe his task to be and so inadequate his ability to execute it. The difficulty of finding proper expression for his ideas kept those ideas in a state of permanent revolution and made him «obsessed» with them. The finished work could not, therefore, be a conventional work of art or intellect; it would be a creation of sheer energy and force, written «a lo que salga» (II, 903). Like Pío Baroja who later claimed that the novel was «un saco donde cabe todo,» Ganivet believed that his creation also embraced broader realms and was not limited to art, history, science, idealism, or naturalism (II, 879).

Yet for all his anguish in writing, Ganivet assured his friend that the labor brought him great pleasure (II, 882-3). And shortly after the book's publication, he referred to its creation as cathartic and indispensable for freeing him from the *impedimenta* of foolish ideas and for enabling him through his novelistic excursion into Africa, to take a bracing plunge into barbarism.[38]

As to the substance of the book, Ganivet early distinguished two principal ingredients: first, a man with an adventurous spirit whose love for his homeland increases the farther from it he travels; and second, a nation (comparable in many ways to Spain) of rational beings, the Mayas, not yet well known to explorers and possessing some constituents of culture but lacking the elements of high civilization, such as industry, commerce, banking, etc. However, as the novel unfolds, the adventurer and Maya become pretexts for an examination of the civilizing innovations that the adventurous Spaniard, Pío Cid (known to the Mayas as Arimi, or «orator» in Maya language), introduces in every field of endeavor, industries, arts, customs, government, etc. It is in the effects of these reforms, Ganivet said, that the book's worth lay, although when he said this a few months into the writing, he was not sure if he trusted himself to maintain the proper balance in tone, which he wanted to be «serio, con tendencia a la guasa, y guasón, con tendencia a la seriedad... y además temo que resulte el pastel con aire extravagante, porque las

[36] *Ibid.*, 56.
[37] Other references to the genesis of *La conquista* in this volume are on: 146, 149, 153, 156, 160, 162, 262, 307, 310, 315. See also *Revista de Occidente*, II (1965), 304-5 and *Obras*, II, 918, 922, 920.
[38] AGUDIEZ, *Las novelas...*, 79-80.

necesidades del asunto me han llevado a tratar materias demasiado ridículas» (II, 905).

From his correspondence it is clear that Ganivet gave much thought to the title of his novel, even though he hoped the perfect title would spring spontaneously to mind. He considered *Canovas-sive-de Restauratione,* after the Prime Minister Antonio Cánovas del Castillo, later assassinated by the anarchist Angiolillo in August of 1897. He also thought he might follow the custom of the poor, who name their children after the saint on whose day they are born. So, if he finished «giving birth» on Saint Roque's day, he would name the book «Don Roque Pérez, astuto viajero andaluz y domador de pueblos salvajes» (II, 901). But the title he finally gave the work was dictated not by prosaic happenstance but chiefly by Ganivet's desire to have a title suggesting the universality of his theme. *El reino de Maya* attains this universality linguistically, with the Sanskrit word *Maya* or illusion.[39]

The title's apparent reference to the pre-Columbian Mayans,[40] is really a misnomer. For Ganivet's subject is the illusions of material progress which Europeans virtually worship and have imposed on backward peoples to the Europeans' advantage and to the «savages'» detriment. Nor is Ganivet's Maya literally the Central American kingdom; Ganivet is talking about Africa and the nineteenth-century conquerors, chiefly the British, French, and Belgians.

Much of Ganivet's information about Africa—its geography, history, ethnography, and languages—probably came from Henry M. Stanley's *Through the Dark Continent* (1878) and *In Darkest Africa* (1890).[41] Ganivet had also read a number of other books on Africa, and in the summer of 1893 he remarked that he continued to read these books because Africa was the continent that he found most congenial (II, 838). In mid-October of 1893 he wrote to Navarro Ledesma that his interest in Africa went far beyond matters of exploration, culture, or colonization. He was idealizing Africa and trying to imagine the role Africa would play in the future of Europe. Foreseeing tremendous growth in the African population as well as in industrial capacity and in the production of raw materials, Ganivet believed Africa would become a mighty competitor of Europe. He even imagined that in two or four centuries Africa might assume world leadership. After all, he said, the European continent received almost all its ideas from Asia, and with these ideas the Europeans established new organizations and stemmed Asiatic expansion. A similar pattern could be repeated by Africa with ideas from Europe.

Ganivet's africanophilism at the time he wrote *La conquista* extended to his urging Spain to establish ties of common interest with Africa—by contrast to the rest of Europe which was bent on merely exploiting the

39 See ROBERT E. OSBORNE, «Observations on Ganivet's *La conquista del reino de Maya,*» *Homenaje a Rodríguez-Moñino* (Madrid, 1966) II, 41-2, and F. GARCÍA LORCA, *Angel Ganivet*..., 35-6.

40 See AGUDIEZ, *Las novelas*..., 78-9.

41 *Ibid.*, 58-70.

Africans. And since Spain lacked the material means of establishing these ties, Ganivet decided to do the job with his pen. Hence *La conquista.*

Ganivet placed his work in the tradition of the histories of the Spanish conquistadors and of the discovery and domination of the Indies (NML, 78) and he intended his character to be a Spanish Robinson Crusoe: «un hombre de acción y de perspicacia, un transformador de hombres» (NML, 78). The work's harsh criticism of human nature and its use of the grotesque as a powerful ironic strategy also link it to the Spanish satirical tradition of Francisco de Quevedo and Francisco Goya, whose *Caprichos* particularly recall *La conquista.* As the story of a traveller in foreign lands whose observations and experiences expose the false superiority of European beliefs and practices and shake the European reader's confidence in the «advanced» state of his civilization, the book owes much to Swift's *Gulliver's Travels,* José Cadalso's *Cartas Marruecas* and the French eighteenth-century tradition of travel literature, notably Montesquieu's *Lettres persanes* and Voltaire's *Candide.* Conrad's *Heart of Darkness* (1902), written not long after *La conquista,* also belongs to this tradition.[42]

The novel, a first person narration, after the fact, of the adventures of an enterprising young Spaniard, Pío Cid, in Maya, an African kingdom previously unknown to Europeans, consists of twenty-two chapters and an epilogue: «Sueño de Pío Cid.» Chapters I and II describe the protagonist, Pío Cid, whose biography has much in common with that of his creator —both are from Andalusia, suffer life-threatening accidents in childhood, obtain law degrees and decline to go into the family business—and how he becomes an explorer in Africa, where he is captured, but is able to escape.

Chapter II closes with Pío Cid astride a hippopotamus that he has discovered on a river bank. The animal is equipped with a bridle and saddlebags, and as the two set off Pío Cid characterizes himself as «el más original caballero andante que se haya visto en el mundo» (I, 332). The allusion to the Spanish novels of chivalry, and particularly to Cervantes' great parody of them in the figure of Don Quixote and his nag Rocinante is obvious. Like Don Quixote, Pío Cid is an idealist at odds with society who will try, perhaps more successfully than his sixteenth-century predecessor, to impose his ideals on that society.

In the following chapter Pío Cid, mounted on the hippopotamus, arrives in a settlement where, much to his surprise, he is greeted with great enthusiasm by its inhabitants, who call him Igana Iguru, «man from on high.» Pío Cid distrusts this enthusiasm, since he knows how fickle crowds can be. But as it turns out, he has been mistaken for

[42] See JEAN FRANCO, «Ganivet and the Technique of Satire in *La conquista del reino de Maya,*» *Bulletin of Hispanic Studies,* XLII (1965), 34-5, and AGUDIEZ, *Las novelas...,* 81-90, for an analysis of the Swiftian elements in *La conquista.* A study of the similarities and differences between Joseph Conrad's *Heart of Darkness* and *La conquista* has yet to be done.

the Igana Iguru, the high priest and judge whose hippopotamus he rides. And he quickly assumes the Igana Iguru's role.

Pío Cid's first case in this new position provides Ganivet an occasion to poke fun at the legal practices of contemporary European democracy. Swift and even Lewis Carroll come to mind as Pío Cid, mounted on the hippo as a kind of travelling tribunal, must determine if an ass or its owner is to be punished for the desecration of the *tembé* where offerings are made to Rubango, the leading Maya deity. Both defendants appear with legal counsel, and the whole procedure most impresses Pío Cid, for he discovers that the Mayas possess juristic practices and principles which the most advanced European experts would heartily endorse: the equality of all beings (including the ass) before the law and a people's jury «conforme a los sanos principios de la más pura democracia» (I, 338).

Yet his verdict is a harsh one: he condemns the man to death. He does so because he perceives that the crowd wants blood and by giving it to them he will gain their respect. Although he feels momentary compassion for the poor prisoner whose head is swiftly chopped off, he rationalizes his decision by assigning all responsibility for it to the angry crowd. This stance is typical of Pío Cid throughout the novel as he refuses to accept any responsibility for the negative effects of his policies, although Ganivet makes the reader clearly aware of those effects. Yet in this case Ganivet does not so much blame Pío Cid as the public: finding an easy victim, the people demand his death to assuage their religious fears and satisfy their blood lust. Thus does democracy subvert justice.

The following eighteen chapters of the novel largely describe the «reforms» that Pío Cid as Igana Iguru initiates in Maya. Maya society before Pío Cid's reign has much in common with pre-nineteenth-century Spain. But some of its values and customs also serve to satirize the Europe and Spain of Ganivet's time.[43] The Swiftian satire of the procedure by which Maya court office seekers are appointed *Uagangas* or counselors to the throne and how they must behave to maintain these posts reflects the low esteem in which Ganivet held contemporary Spain's parliamentary government. As in *Gulliver's Travels,* aspirants to office must perform ridiculous dances, exercises, and animal imitations before a King who is such a cypher he is said to be a «made to order» constitutional monarch. Further, a close examination reveals the main qualification for office is no more than kinship to the royal family. Not that qualifications matter much, for once appointed they have no responsibilities since the King ignores them.[44]

Ganivet also satirizes the Spanish educational system and its competitive exams—recalling Ganivet's failure two years earlier to obtain the chair in Greek at the University of Granada—by means of the Maya educational system and the self-delusion it fosters. Teachers teach nothing

[43] MIGUEL OLMEDO MORENO, *El pensamiento de Ganivet* (Madrid, 1966), 160-79, interprets the novel as the history of Europe in the past seven centuries.
[44] See FRANCO, «Ganivet and the Technique of Satire...,» 34-5.

but reading, writing, natural history, and, most importantly, Maya history, which is preeminent because it helps arouse the enthusiasm of the masses and encourages the nation's citizenry to «olvidar las miserias del presente con el recuerdo de las grandezas del pasado» (I, 340). Education in Maya, as in Spain, thus promoted a false patriotism.

Maya and Spain are also similar, to their discredit, in having authoritarian monotheistic national religions that experienced the upheaval of the Counter-Reformation yet maintained many of their earlier traditions. The Maya religion devotes itself to placating the god Rubango, who personifies evil. But Rubango's character is significantly altered by Pío Cid in his guise of Arimi, the high priest reportedly murdered twenty years earlier whose identity the Spaniard has assumed. He explains to the credulous Mayas that he has spent the intervening years in the subterranean mansions of Rubango and is able to discern the desires of the deity, which, he says, now incline toward progress and change, rather than against them as previously. The innovations that Pío Cid subsequently introduces in Maya thus have the approval of Rubango, which greatly facilitates their acceptance.

The dogmas of the Maya religion are contained in the books of *Kim,* which resemble the old and new Testaments in that they contain an account of the origins of Maya society and establish the purposes of Maya tradition. The *Kim* also satirize the Judeo-Christian tradition and nineteenth-century pieties. The first *Kim,* for example, parodies the Biblical account of the creation by telling of the simultaneous appearance of pairs of animals of all the species except human beings, which are merely foreshadowed by monkeys. The second *Kim,* as related by Pío Cid, is an amalgam of two myths: the tower of Babel and Icarus. In it the Igana Nioniyi climbs to the top of a pyramid built to observe the heavens; fitted with wings he is inflated to the size of a hippopotamus and he disappears in the sky, never to return. The third *Kim* records that the Igana Nioniyi arrived in a heaven inhabited by clever monkeys, who become his slaves and with whom he mates, producing a race known as *cabilis.* The Igana Nioniyi decides to send the new race to the earth to work for mankind. Since the Mayas believe that the *cabilis* will create the perfect society on earth, they seek to hasten their benefactors' arrival by ingratiating themselves with the Igana Nioniyi. As Franco has observed, this myth satirizes the nineteenth-century ideal of exalted individualism and Social Utopia and demonstrates again how Ganivet transforms «into grotesque myths the most cherished assumptions of his age.»[45] But Ganivet is also, obviously, poking fun here at the Christian belief that Christ rose into heaven and that He will inaugurate a beatific age when He returns.

Satiric as is Ganivet's portrait of primitive Maya society, the thrust of Ganivet's criticism is directed at the «modern» reforms introduced by Pío Cid. For he finds the Mayas «felices como bestias» and then through his reforms, innovations and «progress» on the European model, he makes

45 *Ibid.,* 39-40.

them, in the words of Hernán Cortés in the final pages of the book, «desgraciados como hombres» (I, 650).

When Pío Cid arrives in Maya he observes a tranquility rooted in a contented domestic life that even he admires. And he confesses that although the social life of Maya's cities could not satisfy him, the pleasures of domestic life could make him forget his homeland for months at a time. For the Mayas, these pleasures are no incidental escape; they are a product of stringent social rules. The Maya working day ends at nightfall; the city gates are closed until dawn and no one is permitted to enter or leave the city until the next day. Peace and quiet reign; the streets are dark, there is no theatre, there are no cafes nor any other public meeting places. The men, who have spent the daylight hours exclusively in the company of other men, return home where they spend the next six hours in the company of their large families.

The women of Maya spend their days in the women's quarters or gynaeceum, unless they have been sentenced to work in the fields because of sloth. They happily weave esparto grass for clothing, nurse their young, and sing the praises of a man—a husband, father, or son depending on their circumstances. Yet they are viewed as little more than domestic animals, being required to love the way animals are required to work (I, 342). And should a woman prove to be sterile she is returned to her former family, which must return half of the price received for her. She can only avoid this punishment if she is beautiful and therefore able to enter a very rich man's harem as a woman of luxury.

Pío Cid views polygamy as a social institution beneficial to all, particularly in a place such as Maya where women greatly outnumber men. Polygamy, he claims, protects women from economic misery and prevents them from becoming prostitutes. It also solves a social problem that goes unsolved in more advanced societies: women must stay at home to fulfill their mission as mothers and child-rearers, yet they also need the company of other women of their class and interests. In Europe this conflict is rarely resolved happily; some women become housebound prisoners while others abandon their homes for the theater, or for their friends' homes. The Mayas have the perfect solution. In the gynaeceum women can fulfill the inherent aspirations of their sex and enjoy appropriate companionship and still have a protector for themselves and their children.

Ganivet's evident sanction of polygamy, as well as of polyandry which is practiced in the poorer areas of Maya, was not confined to the pages of his novel. He wrote to Navarro in June of 1893, for instance, that polygamy and polyandry are far superior to monogamy,

> con la cual únicamente pueden existir y existen, al lado de las señoras encopetadas, que nos tratan, aunque seamos sus maridos, como a criados o mozos de cuerda, las bandas cerradas e innumerables de prostitutas y el cúmulo de incidencias que de éstas se deriva. (II, 841)

In another letter four years later, April 12, 1897, he concedes the unconventionality of his ideas in *La conquista* and defends his satirical way of presenting them by asking «¿Cómo voy a defender directamente la poligamia y demás ideas absurdas que tengo la desgracia de profesar?»[46]

The practice of polygamy is not the only oddity of Maya family life that promotes tranquility. Another is the acceptance of adultery. Adulterous unions are only condemned when the male is of a lower class than the husband. In fact, if the male is of a higher class, the act becomes an advantage to the family and is called *yosimiré,* which means «notable favor» (I, 348). Children born of these irregular unions are actually prized since it is assumed that they were conceived on a religious day, the only day of the month when the Maya women can leave their homes and appear in public. Children born to unmarried women are also well regarded since the chastity of young women is not of much importance to the Mayas, and usually the father marries the mother either out of love of self interest; because such children are financially valuable, the males can be sold as servants and the females as wives. Hence, in Maya fathers do not fail to acknowledge their illegitimate children.

One wonders whether Ganivet's unusual marriage customs in *La conquista* are not in some way a reflection of his own dissatisfactions with the traditional relations between the sexes and his own failure or inability to create an enduring and satisfying family. This is a theme to which Ganivet will return in *Los trabajos* and it is one which has not been paid sufficient critical attention.

The outstanding feature of the Maya government at the time of Pío Cid's arrival is its stability, a quality the new Arimi fully appreciates and which he seeks to maintain in a number of ways. The chief of these is the creation of new classes of government functionaries whose loyalty to their employer is to be insured by satisfying their self-interest. Pío Cid hit upon this idea after learning of the savvy King Usana who kept his subjects faithful by distributing some of his wealth and by creating the Assembly of *Uagangas* and the Corps of Educators to employ the more ambitious citizens who might otherwise conspire against the state if not granted some influence in its affairs. He also orchestrated a certain animosity between the army and the populace, which he hopes will control the ambitions and discontent of both. He takes his cue for this kind of government from the Maya chronicle that Pío Cid quotes on more than one occasion and that recalls the views Ganivet expressed in letters he wrote from Antwerp during this period.

The Maya chronicle records that in the past, despite the King's greatness, the people suffered, although they suffered with peaceful resignation. Pío Cid understands this to mean that governments cannot remake human nature nor can they legislate the happiness of their subjects. «La felicidad humana,» he says, «no existe, o si existe hay que buscarla por otro camino que por el de los caminos de ley» (I, 397). Thus, despite his political ambition, Pío Cid feels the same kind of pessimism about

[46] «Epistolario...,» *Revista de Occidente,* XI (1965), 305-6. AGUDIEZ, *Las novelas...,* 70.

human life and about the ultimate futility of government as Ganivet expressed to Navarro in his letter of August 18, 1893 (II, 87): government can do little to improve the human condition.[47] We notice again the pessimism of the author and his clear identification with the character.

Pío Cid's pessimism is soon confirmed when a group of «malcontents» who have been excluded from power (largely servants, untenured educators, and farmers who wanted permanent land grants) and who advocate an egalitarian system diametrically opposed to Pío Cid's elitist system, take over the government. The revolutionaries dismantle the cities and grant each family a plot where they are to live autonomously until the arrival of the mythical *cabilis* puts an end to human toil. But even this regime is doomed. For in a satiric swipe at male egalitarian idealists, Ganivet has the new system fall because it disrupts the monthly observance of the religious ceremonies which were the only occasions when the women were allowed to participate in society —and to engage in free sexual activity. This episode provides Ganivet with the opportunity to ridicule the popular utopian solutions which sought to redistribute the land but neglected to attend to the other important issues in society, such as the position of women in a social order that responds only to male concerns.

It is not surprising that a disgruntled woman assassinates the Igana Iguru who replaced Pío Cid and sets in motion a brief and bloody revolution that culminates in the restoration of the legitimist monarchy with Pío Cid as Igana Iguru, under Mujanda, the new king, an incompetent, irresponsible, pleasure seeker.[48]

Distressed by the demoralization in Maya after so much political upheaval and recognizing the incompetence and irresponsibility of the governing class (which, again, recalls its Spanish counterpart), Pío Cid takes the affairs of government into his own hands in order to insure the continuity of King Mujanda (and himself) in power. He gives humanitarian and scientific reasons for his actions, but it is clear that he is far from disinterested, desiring to maintain his position.[49] He sees the necessity and yet the difficulty of maintaining a delicate balance among the various constituencies of the realm, and he realizes once again that «la felicidad de un pueblo es cosa imposible de conseguir» (II, 444). He decides to stabilize the situation by unifying and centralizing the government and by granting the different interest groups equal and even larger interests in the affairs of state. Paper money and centrally administered taxes are among the first innovations. Then follows a three-pronged reform which enormously increases the number of civil servants, army

[47] OLMEDO MORENO, *El pensamiento...*, 149 and 179, note 1, points out the relationship of these views to those of Humboldt.

[48] These episodes, as D. L. SHAW has poited out *(The Generation of 1898...*, 33) resemble the Federalist revolts in southern and eastern Spain in 1873. Ganivet's attendance at a Parisian production of *Lysistrata* in May of 1883 (II, 835-6) may also have contributed to this section.

[49] See FRANCO, «Ganivet and the Technique of Satire...,» 38, for a discussion of the parody of Spencer.

personnel and members of the Assembly of Uagangas. Promotion lists ranked according to seniority are created and consequently a new form of self-seeking ambition appears in Maya since now every male citizen can aspire to fill all posts, except that of King.

The result of these reforms is rampant bribery and corruption and a bureaucracy akin to the one that so burdened nineteenth-century Spain. The narrator defends this swollen bureaucracy on the grounds that the only faithful defenders of the government are the useless officials whose self-interest makes them eager to protect their positions and who suspect that any unrest is motivated by those who wish to replace them. Characteristically, neither social institutions nor human nature escape the sting of Ganivet's satire. This ironic emphasis on bureaucratic self-interest as the bulwark of the state reflects the Spanish vice-consul's worries over his own promotion and his distaste for the importance of professional rank, which, he believed, devoured all self respect, professionalism, and interior motivations (II, 921).

The last five chapters of the novel are largely a chronicle of the growth of Maya's material civilization. Under the direction of Pío Cid, the nation undergoes a major revolution of industry and commerce brought about by his desire to create a national structure in which the interdependency of the diverse elements is so great that the structure itself, and thus the national unity of Maya, will endure permanently. To insure this he introduces a new governmental monopoly —on alcohol. His justification for the act is pure Ganivetean satire. He says he had observed that the prosperity of European nations seemed to depend above all on the reduction of their citizens to the level of animals, all for the greater glory and wealth of society. Now Pío Cid decides to strengthen Maya by brutalizing its citizens not only through spiritless work and mindless materialism but through the stupefactions of alcohol.

The consequences of these policies are quickly apparent. A cash economy is established, a division of labor emerges which necessitates merchants, the law of supply and demand takes hold, commerce, industry and technology flourish, even in previously poor areas of the country (paralleling the growth of such Spanish industrial cities as Barcelona and Bilbao), and people drink themselves numb —numb to pain, numb to politics, numb to life.

Yet a certain restlessness runs throughout Maya society giving rise to the arts and sciences. Sculpture, music, and drama flower in spite of the prevalent dissipation. Architecture, natural history, geography, astronomy, and medicine advance. The reader, however, is not informed as to how one citizen becomes a drunk while another an artist or a scientist. The author leaves us with the inference that the human spirit will always extricate itself from total degradation. Both art and science are avenues through which the creative impulse can escape the predominant barbarism of human society.

Although art and science provide outlets for the Mayas, religion is perverted into a handmaiden of commercial society. The cynical Pío Cid sets up a highly lucrative industry at a holy site —the manufacture and sale of religious items. Ganivet's evident target here is not so much religious superstition as the commercial exploiting of religion. Ganivet saw this happening all around him, and in October 1895 he published an article, «Lecturas extranjeras,» on Zola's *Lourdes* and Pierre Loti's *Jerusalem* in *El Defensor,* condemning the commercialization of Lourdes and the Holy Land. (The original tone of the article was apparently so strong that the piece was revised during the summer of 1895 by Nicolás María López to make it acceptable for publication.)[50] There he laments the appropriation of Bernadette's sincere faith by a flock of commercial enterprises that exploit those who truly believe. He is also horrified by the European tourist hotels across from the church of the Nativity in Bethlehem and by a sign advertising: «Fulano de tal, fabricante de artículos de devoción a precios reducidos» (I, 972). Ganivet sees in these prostitutions of religion instances of the inhumanly commercial «modern spirit» and of the latest generation of the merchants Jesus threw out of the temple. Not only the faithful raise their voices against this mob, says Ganivet, but also those like Loti, and probably Ganivet himself, who bemoan their own lost faith. The article ends with the affirmation that faith should not be extirpated from the human heart even if it be illusion, because it can calm and sooth the pain of existence (I, 973). In this respect, although in a different tone, Ganivet's defense of unquestioning religious faith parallels Unamuno's vindication of *la fe del carbonero* and anticipates his own more extensive elaboration of the theme in *Los trabajos del infatigable creador, Pío Cid.*

In *La conquista,* Ganivet's satire of the commercial exploitation of religion also points toward the appreciation of innocent faith hinted at in «Lecturas extranjeras.» At the death of King Mujanda his 155 wives willingly sacrifice themselves to follow their master. The value of sacrificing oneself for an ideal, in this case a marital one, rather than becoming attached to material goods, is emphasized toward the end of the novel in the sections written some two years after the rest of the book.[51]

In the chapter preceding the epilogue, Pío Cid, en route to Spain, and on the verge of death from a tropical fever, encounters an Englishman, a proselytizing protestant, who despoils him of virtually all his belongings. This unnamed figure, ironically called "el misionero o comerciante,» exemplifies the worthlessness of an ideal which is so impure as to be allied with ordinary self interest.[52] «¿Quién,» asks Pío, «será tan menguado que se imagine a Jesús explicando alguna de sus admirables parábolas y sacando luego un variado surtido de baratijas para venderlas a

[50] The revised article was published October 4, 1895, although the *Obras* indicates it was October 5. See GM:ET, 52-5, for the original version. See MARIE LAFFRANQUE, «A Propos de *Lourdes* d'Emile Zola: Angel Ganivet et le christianisme contemporain,» *Bulletin Hispanique,* LXIX (1967), 6-84, for a carefully documented discussion of Ganivet's relation to Christianity.

[51] AGUDIEZ, *Las novelas...*, 55-6.

[52] The model for this character may have been Charles Henry Stokes, a British missionary who became a highly successful ivory trader and was executed by a Belgian officer early in 1895. See S. J. S. COOKEY, *Britain and the Congo Question, 1885-1913* (London, 1968), 31-4.

buen precio a sus oyentes?» (I, 640). Jesus is ennobled by his sacrifice, which makes him worthy of the faith humanity has placed in him.[53]

The theme of disinterested sacrifice is presented again in the book's epilogue, the allegorical «Sueño de Pío Cid.» In his «Sueño,» Pío Cid, back in Spain and employed in an insignificant bureaucratic post meets Hernán Cortés, who urges him to publish his memoirs of his experiences in Maya. In response to Pío Cid's protestations that his conquests and discoveries have brought no benefit to him or his homeland and not even a change in the maps, Cortés points out that Pío Cid's conquests are not of use to Spain, nor should they be, but that they are glorious in themselves and, besides, they have not required excessive expenditures.

Anticipating Ganivet's view in the *Idearium* that Spain's failure to obtain lasting material benefits from her once magnificent colonial empire is actually a sign of spiritual strength, Cortés tells Pío Cid:

> Los grandes pueblos y los grandes hombres, pobres han sido, son y serán; y las empresas más grandiosas son aquellas en que no interviene el dinero, en que los gastos recaen exclusivamente sobre el cerebro y el corazón. (I, 648)

He also praises Pío Cid for his selflessness, which makes his efforts all the more beautiful since ultimately his sojourn in Maya did not enrich him materially. In response to Pío Cid's lingering concern over his participation in the sacrifice of Mujanda's 155 wives, Cortés states that the fundamental legal principle should be not the right to life but the right to an ideal, even at the expense of one's life. He firmly disapproves of the sacrifice of human lives if the motives are petty. But the sacrifice of Mujanda's wives for the sake of conjugal fidelity ennobles their existence. «Amable es la vida, pero ¿cuánto más amable no es el ideal a que podemos elevarnos sacrificándola?» (I, 652).

The «Sueño» lends the novel an association with Spain's great literary and colonial past. Near the beginning Pío Cid had been compared to Don Quixote. At the end he is compared to Hernán Cortés, and he is praised for his idealism and generosity in bringing civilization to Maya, unlike the often brutal conquests carried out by the conquistador. Cortés even suggests that perhaps Spain would have been better off if she had reserved for herself the glory of her heroic undertakings and had left to other, more practical nations «la misión de poblar las tierras descubiertas y conquistadas y el cuidado de todos los bajos menesteres de la colonialización» (I, 648).

Thus despite the satire that enfolds Pío Cid's misplaced reformism —the negative effects of material progress, the destruction of the harmonious Maya family, the corruption and drunkenness of the Mayas— Ganivet admires Pío Cid's efforts and idealism as a nineteenth-century Quixote and allows Cortés to praise Pío Cid's civilizing measures as the «levadura» that lifts the Mayas' spirit (I, 651). Civilized man «halla su dicha en el esfuerzo doloroso que le exige su propia liberación,» Cortés says,

[53] This same idea is found in *Idearium* (I, 45).

«conquistar, colonizar, civilizar no es, pues, otra cosa que infundir el amor al esfuerzo que dignifica al hombre, arrancándole del estado de ignorante quietud en que viviría eternamente» (I, 650). Here Ganivet represents civilization not as decadence but as rewarding effort and labor[54] just as José Ortega y Gasset was to do later in *La rebelión de las masas.*

At the end Pío Cid emerges from his catastrophic adventures as a spiritual hero, and Cortés envisions destroying the civilized nations so that he might witness the blossoming of a new human ideal from their ruins. "En el paso de la barbarie a la civilización se encuentran siempre las mayores crueldades de nuestras historias» (I, 653). The note of proto-fascism sounds here, but by Cortés' reasoning, Pío Cid did more good than harm in Maya: by undermining the old culture he prepared the way for a new and superior one —albeit not the one he first had in mind (I, 653). Thus, the «Sueño» represents Ganivet's final evaluation of what Pío Cid has achieved in Maya and an idealistic view of a future in which destruction of imperfection will lead to superior creation.[55]

Underscoring this idea, Ganivet explained to Navarro that the heart of the novel lay in the story of a lone man of great energy and few material desires who enters a somnolent, backward society and through his labors, which serve as a ferment, brings that society to life. This interpretation comes as something of a surprise after the generally negative, satiric portrayal of Pío Cid's activities as the novel unfolds. It is as though Ganivet's view of the book changed in the course of the writing. Ganivet hinted at such a change not long after the work was finished when he wrote Navarro: «la deducción está en el *Sueño,* que a mi juicio es lo único que vale en la obra y lo que me ha decidido a publicarla.»[56]

Yet the reader is left perplexed by the realignment of the work which the «Sueño» imposes. The initial banal ending which finds Pío Cíd back in Spain, an orphan (Ganivet finished *La conquista* in the four months following his mother's death), his days spent in bureaucratic drudgery for despicable superiors, is appropriately deflating and suggests that Pío's African adventures were the fantasy of an obscure *funcionario.* However, the identification of Ganivet with Pío Cid makes it necessary that the character's existence possess greater resonance than that afforded in this perhaps for Ganivet all too real and anticlimactic ending. The «Sueño,» therefore, by relating Pío Cid in an extraordinary way to a grandiose and approving national hero, denies the insignificance of his character and of himself.

As the year 1895 drew toward its own ending, Ganivet put the final

[54] GONZALO SOBEJANO, «Ganivet o la soberbia,» similarly finds this the end result of Pío Cid's influence in Maya.

[55] Again, in April of 1897, «Epistolario...,» *Revista de Occidente,* XI (1965), 305, Ganivet wrote to Navarro that he believed in destruction as a means of regaining human ideals: «¿Cómo voy a defender sobre todo los sacrificios humanos que yo creo que hacen grandísima falta?... Si yo expusiera mis ideas con claridad, me meterían en la cárcel... creo que hace falta en España levadura fresca y que alguien ha de llevarla.»

[56] AGUDIEZ, *Las novelas...,* 77.

touches to two of his major occupations: his work on *La conquista,* completed in December, and his service as vice consul in Antwerp. In late December he learned of his promotion to consul second class in Helsinki. The thirty-year-old who boarded the train in Antwerp was not yet a recognized author, although he had begun to write seriously. But in less than three years, having produced, in a flurry of creation, all his major works, he was to be a writer of stature. Leaving Antwerp seems to have been a boon to his work. The Belgian city appears to have afflicted Ganivet with a debilitating sense of alienation. He once remarked to Navarro Ledesma that he had kept his clothes and papers in a suitcase ever since his arrival in Antwerp so that in fifteen minutes he could be at the railroad station without having left behind more than two or three old hats and several pairs of old shoes. And he considered the different rooms he lived in there merely «bancos públicos donde uno se sienta para descansar un momento» (II, 1001).

Ganivet's journey to Helsinki took him eastward through Germany; he stopped in Berlin for a few days, was impressed by the number of military men and the variety of uniforms but oppressed by the noisiness of trains, carriages, hotels, and restaurants and by the cult of the Kaiser, whose visage he encountered everywhere peering down from sculptured busts. He found Königsberg, the former capital of Prussia, much more congenial. Neither modern, noisy, or active, it seemed at a standstill, secure in its ancient character and its integrity (CFAG, 268-9). After a quick stop in Saint Petersburg, Ganivet arrived at his destination in the former Russian Grand Duchy of Finland, where he assumed his new position on February 1, 1896.

CHAPTER 3

HELSINKI

During the two and a half years Ganivet spent in Helsinki, from early 1896 until the summer of 1898, he produced an extraordinary flow of literary work; and he began to establish a considerable reputation for himself, especially in Granada. In this short time he wrote *Granada la bella, Cartas finlandesas, Idearium español, Hombres del norte,* and *Los trabajos del infatigable creador, Pío Cid.*

«*Granada la bella*»

Since the port of Helsinki remained frozen until May, the new consul had few diplomatic tasks to perform during the initial period of his residency. The long, fierce winter created a feeling of isolation and nostalgia for Spain that could be tempered by writing:

> ¿Qué va uno a hacer aquí, en días como el de hoy, en que desde la mesa donde escribo, ... veo cruzar, desencadenados, horribles huracanes de nieve, que parecen anuncio del juicio final? ... Y a ratos ni siquiera tengo la tranquilidad de defenderme, acurrucado en mi pequeña casa, porque temo salir volando con ella, e ir a parar al quinto infierno. No queda, pues, más recurso que amorrarse, coger la pluma y escribir ... (NML, 59)

On February 14, scarcely a fortnight after his arrival in Helsinki, Ganivet began a series of articles on Granada for *El Defensor*. Composing one article every day, except Sundays, he finished the last one, the twelfth, on February 27, and the Granada newspaper published them between February 29 and April 13 under the title *Granada la bella* (CFAG, 276).[1]

Essentially a short treatise on urban aesthetics, and a paean to the city of his birth, *Granada la bella* was written while Ganivet was living in a neighborhood that suggested Granada: Brunsparken, «the best of Helsinki,» a sort of Finnish equivalent of the setting of the Alhambra,

[1] LSLP, 87, and NML, 66, indicate that Ganivet destroyed two articles because he thought them «too personal.» He later wrote another article which is included in GALLEGO BURÍN's 1954 edition of *Granada la bella,* 165-7, but which is not in his *Obras.*

laid in a forest surrounded by the sea and dotted with wooden chalets.

The idea of writing a book about Granada came to Ganivet in consequence of his visit there in August of 1895, following the death of his mother (when published anonymously in book form, the work was dedicated to her), and his visit to Bruges, in the fall of that same year.[2] The two cities provided Ganivet with a dramatic contrast in response to historical change: while Bruges had, according to Ganivet, admirably preserved its traditional communal spirit against the pressures of commerce and industry, Granada seemed to Ganivet to have succumbed to modernization. This ill fate was signalled in 1895 by the opening of the *Gran vía* which stretched from the center of the city to the outskirts on a course that had meant the destruction of a picturesque labyrinth of twisting Moorish streets, arab palaces and renaissance buildings representing the fusion of Moorish and Christian culture in Granada. Ganivet wrote *Granada la bella* in part to protest this ruinous highway and to support the efforts of like-minded *granadinos* to save the city's aesthetic character from the wrecker's ball.

Drawing upon his cosmopolitan experience as well as upon the Spanish literary tradition of *costumbrismo,* Ganivet assumes in *Granada la bella* the point of view of a loyal and loving native son who urges his fellow *granadinos* to cherish local traditions rather than to imitate the practices of other nations. Writing in a frank, unpretentious, conversational style, he proposes to put forth «ideas viejas con espíritu nuevo, y acaso ideas nuevas con viejo espíritu» (I, 61) in addressing the serious problem of how cities in general, and Granada in particular, should adapt to historical change. As he had done in *La conquista,* Ganivet again stresses the priority of spiritual vitality over material gains. He even cautioned against the introduction of such innovations as a sewer system and running water. What mattered, he said, was the interior cleansing of the individual, not the exterior cleansing of streets and homes. And if modern plumbing were installed, the city would lose the charming *aguadores,* and the rite of buying from them, which Ganivet believed to represent an element of Granadan spirit that, despite the inconvenience, must be preserved.

Ganivet also stresses the importance of local traditions in the development of a city's architecture and the need to respect buildings suited to specific sites. Granada's architecture, he observed, typically intermingles man-made constructions with plants and flowers, affording both beauty and protection from the summer heat. Thus low houses, cooler than those rising into the sun, possess refreshing flower and plant filled patios, and they lie along narrow, twisting streets that provide valuable shade. To destroy these houses and streets and replace them with multistory dwellings and wide, straight avenues like those of northern cities would work to the detriment of life in Granada for the sake of an imitative

[2] He also read GEORGE RODENBACH'S *Bruges la morte* which may have contributed to his desire to write about Granada. See FERNÁNDEZ ALMAGRO'S *Introducción* to GANIVET'S *Obras completas,* 28-9. Ganivet comments on Rodenbach in II, 985.

modernity —and at the cost of having to accept the monotony of the modern city as well.[3]

The central article of *Granada la bella,* both structurally and thematically, is «Nuestro carácter.» In its attempt to define the character of the *granadino,* and by extension to give a brief assessment of traits shared by all Spaniards, it anticipates *Idearium español,*[4] which he had apparently begun at the time. The essay's specific purpose is to distinguish between the true assimilation of foreign influences and the vulgar imitation of elements alien to the city's or the nation's true character.

The fundamental characteristic of the Spanish people in general, and of the citizens of Granada in particular (thanks to their Christian and Arabic ancestry), Ganivet asserts, is mysticism. All the peculiarities of Spanish life stem from this trait. Spain's failure to establish lasting commercial enterprises and her success in founding enduring religious communities are both fruits of mysticism. For Spaniards can understand and institute community property when the goal is an idealistic one, but they do not know how to organize capital to make it prosper. «Nuestra fuerza está en nuestro ideal con nuestra pobreza,» Ganivet writes, «no en la riqueza sin ideales» (I, 98).

Ganivet enlists the same cause to explain Spain's lack of accomplishment in applied science —the failure to invent any notable machine or discover any new planets or microbes. But, like Unamuno, who exclaimed, «Qué inventen ellos,» Ganivet does not consider this lack a shortcoming. In a passage that recalls the spiritual message of *La conquista,* Ganivet dismisses Spain's insignificance in science by pointing with pride to the historic valor and conquests of the Spaniards as well as to their great art, their faith, and their mystic wisdom. After having excelled in these regions of the ideal, he says, the Spanish mind cannot find such activities as classifying the ridges of the brain, either stimulating or satisfying. The true Spanish science, Ganivet claims, could never take the form of the «second rate» science that now occupies public attention; rather it is to be found in mysticism itself. He points to Miguel Serveto's quite offhanded announcement of his discovery of the circulation of blood in a theological treatise as an example of the Spanish preference for more exalted fare. Firsthand observations of international scientific meetings, in which Spanish representatives are reduced to holding a fourth secretaryship of a section, convinced him of that by disclosing the triviality and vanity of the scientific mind.

Ganivet's deflation of the scientific meeting leads to criticism of the «modern system» of research, which he ridicules by contrasting it with his own method of studying the Spanish character. He says he will not solicit data from the nation's hatters and tailors and the like as a means of

[3] Here again Ganivet closely shares the concern for the monotony and inhumaneness of the city that LITVAK examines in the works of Unamuno, Baroja, Azorín, and Valle-Inclán in *A Dream of Arcadia,* 55-60.

[4] Ganivet's allusion here to a work in progress which deals with «la constitución ideal de la raza española» gives further indication of the connection between the two works.

inducing the average Spanish body type. Such information, he concedes, could have made for a formidable tome which, even though unread, might have brought him academic honors. Instead, he has chosen to employ the old method: living, travelling, and using all five of his senses.[5] The sensations he gathers will arrange themselves and give rise to ideas; the author will then arrange the ideas in a small book that a dozen friends can read without great trouble. And this small book will contain more truth about Spain than dozens of scientific volumes.

Following this article, which ends with another plea for the preservation of Spain's character —let there be no school for telephone operators at the expense of a school of philosophy, he begs— Ganivet turns to Granada's art. Like all Spanish art at its highest level, Ganivet says, Granada's art is inspired by mysticism, although he insists that Granada's writers exhibit an unusual freshness, vigor, and imagination. Classicism, romanticism, orientalism and other foreign currents thus have little to offer the Granadan artist because these currents may violate his natural temperament. According to Ganivet, Granada's genuine art always embodies a mystic idea in a scene of nature. At times this mystical idea is expressed directly, and at other times it is manifested in «un soplo de amor.» Ganivet cites the *granadino* Pedro Antonio de Alarcón's *El sombrero de tres picos* (1874) as a model of what Granada's art should be: «un estudio psicológico bordado en un cuadro de naturaleza» (I, 105).

Ganivet also links the artistic vitality of Granada, or any other city, with the presence of vibrant municipal politics. The cities he most admired —the free cities of Greece, Italy, and the Low Countries— were those whose artistic identities grew alongside their political autonomy, in the absence of a dominating national power. And he took these cities as examples for Granada. In exhorting the *granadinos* to salvage their city's dwindling communal life, he declares that not only will they and Spain benefit materially but, most importantly, this revitalized civic spirit will produce an artistic renaissance. Granada must therefore conserve her municipal freedoms as a necessary condition of her artistic rebirth.[6]

Ganivet's distaste for centralized national governments, so pronounced in the letters and in *La conquista*, also surfaces forcefully in *Granada la bella* in a diatribe against the incompetence of Spain's leaders. Laying the blame at their feet for Spain's failure to assimilate in an appropriate way the benefits of modern civilization such as railroads, Ganivet anticipates the scathing political criticism of Ortega y Gasset's *España invertebrada*. Ganivet complains that the cause of Spain's ills is «la falta de cabeza allí donde debe estar la cabeza» (I, 120). Instead of qualified, knowledgeable

[5] Modern research methods are also deflated in section VIII, «¿Qué somos?», by his statement that statistics can be manipulated to demonstrate whatever one wants, whereas it is in trifling, apparently insignificant observations in which one discovers «el alma de las cosas» (I, 111).

[6] Ganivet's views on regionalism are mostly clearly expressed in his letter of January 26, 1898, to Seco in which he saw the danger of certain regionalist movements' desire for independence and separation from Spain, a goal which he opposed (LSLP, 100-1).

men, Spain has had the misfortune, beginning in the last years of the Hapsburg regime in the seventeenth century, of having ignorant, vain, indolent, and proud men govern her. Ganivet labeled the contemporary version of this type the «hombre de conocimientos generales,» one who is unfit to be an apprentice in any trade and too ignorant to carry out minor duties, and is therefore promoted to high officialdom and entrusted with the most arduous duties of state. He carries out these duties by public sham and behind closed doors plays with paper planes (I, 122).

In contrast to these pretentious charlatans, whom the consul saw in his own superiors, Ganivet set the illiterate citizens, whom he finds here to be honest and courageous, as well as genuinely artistic and philosophical, and whom he credits with having saved Spain from Napoleon when many of the educated citizens were willing to give up Spain's independence (I, 73-4).

Granada la bella closes with a final suggestion for improving the quality of life in Granada: include female citizens in all spheres of civic, professional and cultural activity.[7] The presence of women, he says, will counterbalance the dominance of men and will contribute to the creation of a fully human existence, unlike the «vida de cuartel» that currently prevails.

Although the consul had not yet spent a full month in Helsinki when he wrote this article, he seems to have been immediately impressed by the healthy presence of women in all walks of Finnish life —in the university and the professions, no less than in sales positions, the postal service, banks, and offices. In Helsinki, he remarks, one's sex is an accident that only influences «el vestir y en la elección de algunos oficios que por su naturaleza exigen ya la delicadeza de la mujer, ya la fuerza del hombre» (I, 139). The consul particularly applauds the freedom that the single women of Helsinki enjoy to live independently and honestly by their own labor, without having their reputations thereby sullied, as they would in Spain.

In suggesting that Spanish women participate in Spanish life as fully as their Finnish counterparts, he acknowledges that they must receive training and instruction to prepare them to live independently, and in a traditionalist departure he declares that married women form a separate group whose freedom of movement must necessarily be subordinated to the interests of the family. Half jokingly he adds that if the law assured every young woman a decent husband no woman would give thought to emancipation. Yet in a more serious vein, Ganivet states that women should not make marriage the exclusive goal of their lives; they should not spend their youths dreaming of this single idea; and those who do not marry should not live lives of inaction. Since there are no more

[7] Although he first presents his ideas about the equality of the sexes in a joking tone, one he uses at various times throughout the work, Ganivet was quite serious about his proposal. He wrote to his family in Granada that although these essays may have seemed almost humorous, they had a very serious intention and were not written to make people laugh (CFAG, 284).

knights errant to enchant young damsels, the woman who spends her days waiting for one with no other thought becomes a *ridículo muñeco* (I, 144).[8] With this appeal for civic unity and female ambition and equality, Ganivet closed *Granada la bella.*

Ganivet was impressed not only by the women he observed from a distance actively participating in Helsinki society but also by a number of accomplished women with whom he had sustained personal contact. On March 12, 1896, two weeks after completing *Granada la bella,* Ganivet wrote to Nicolás María López: "Las mujeres son tan libres como los hombres y valen más que los hombres. Existe la amistad entre los dos sexos, sin mezcla de deseos impuros; yo ya tengo una amiga, que es mi profesora de sueco, es decir, una joven rusa, hija de polaco y alemana, con la que sostengo ratos de conversación, y que resulta un tipo rarísimo, comparado con nuestras mujeres» (NML, 61). Ganivet's Swedish teacher was a twenty-five year old widow, Mascha Djakoffsky, «bellísima en el género rubio, pero más seria que un 'chavo de especias'» (NML, 61). This woman clearly widened Ganivet's intellectual horizons. She introduced him to the work of the Norwegians Jonas Lie, Bjornstjerne Bjornson and Henrik Ibsen. She taught him Swedish, helped him perfect his German, and started him on Russian.

Mascha Djakoffsky also touched Ganivet emotionally. She appears to have been the inspiration behind his French poems, the *Pensées melancoliques et sauvages.*[9] And much of his lyric poetry was written during the brief months of his relationship with her from March into the summer of 1896, when Djakoffsky left Helsinki. The end of this friendship seems to have been due in some measure to the jealous presence of Amelia, who arrived in Helsinki in the summer of 1896 and whom Ganivet introduced as his wife. According to Gallego Morell, Ganivet became disconsolate upon Djakoffsky's departure and sought a transfer from Helsinki.[10]

In addition to forming an attachment to his language teacher, Ganivet also acquired a circle of female friends with whom he met regularly. Among them was the painter Hanna Rönnberg, who lived in the same building as Ganivet, the three Wennerbergin sisters, who were close neighbors, and a fifth woman friend, Ella Sahlberg. These women were struck by Ganivet's introverted, unsociable nature, but also drawn, paradoxically, by his conversation. Rönnberg, who did a portrait of the author in December of 1896, remembered Ganivet as «una extraña mezcla de sacerdote árabe y egipcio.»[11]

[8] These comments bring to mind FEDERICO GARCÍA LORCA'S 1935 play, *Doña Rosita la soltera,* in which the lyrical and tragic dimensions of this element of a *granadina*'s existence are explored.

[9] These poems are not in *Obras.* A selection has been published by JUAN DEL ROSAL in *Angel Ganivet: Poesias* (Barcelona, 1940). GALLEGO MORELL has published an edition of Ganivet's poetry written in French, «Poemas en francés de Angel Ganivet,» *Revista de Occidente,* II (1965), 356-71. See also MELCHOR FERNÁNDEZ ALMAGRO, «La poesía de Ganivet,» *Insula,* 228-9, November-December 1965: 1, 24-5; there is a photograph of Djakoffsky on p. 24.

[10] *Angel Ganivet...*, 132-3.

[11] *Ibid.*, 128.

Regardless of the emotional and intellectual rewards and disappointments that Ganivet found in his Finnish friends, most of his energies were devoted to solitary intellectual pursuits: writing, and when he tired, reading in French, English, German, and Swedish. He seems to have been unconcerned by the faint public response aroused by *Granada la bella,* which failed to inspire even one article in the press. His friends López, Navarro, Matías Méndez Vellido and Ruiz de Almodóbar were enthusiastic about the essays and urged Ganivet to publish them in book form, which he did in August of 1896.

Once finished with *Granada la bella,* Ganivet moved on to other, different projects. In early May of 1896 he sent some of his *Pensées melancoliques et sauvages* to López and discussed his desire to publish *La conquista.* But he is concerned that he has not yet found the most fruitful direction for his writing:

> Ya ves cuán lejos estoy ya de *Granada la bella,* idealmente hablando; y ahora que me dices que la cosa ha parecido buena, casi lo siento, por lo mismo que he abandonado esa ruta, que quizás era la mejor. Yo estoy condenado a pasar la vida haciendo ensayos como los cómicos, sólo que a mí no me llega el día de la representación. (NML, 65)

Such doubts, although they troubled Ganivet for the remainder of his life, did not apparently impede his productivity. He soon resumed work on a book he had probably started in Antwerp, a book on ideology which he told López was «mejor que lo que hace [Unamuno]» (NML, 69) and which held the highest place among all his works in their author's eyes—*Idearium español.*

«*Idearium español*»

Idearium español fills only 155 pages of the complete works of Ganivet, which run to just over 2,000 pages. Yet despite its brevity, the book carries great ambitions. For, expanding upon insights sketched in *Granada la bella* and on conceptions underlying *España filosófica contemporánea,* Ganivet here presents a comprehensive and eminently flattering interpretation of the Spanish *Volksgeist* and uncompromising advice on how to achieve national regeneration by turning inward, cultivating spirituality, and rejecting the example of materialism offered by other, only superficially more successful nations.

Completed in October of 1896 and published the following summer, the *Idearium,* despite some initial delay in receiving favorable critical attention, won the praise of several important critics even before the author's death a little over a year after the book's publication. Ganivet's tragic and mysterious suicide on November 29, 1898, coincident with momentous historical events, then insured the book wide notice. Ganivet's loyal and enthusiastic friends and admirers, in particular Navarro Ledesma, by then a well-known writer in Madrid, and Nicolás María López, published obituaries in the major Madrid newspapers bearing glowing appreciations of their dead companion's works. Thus, shortly after Spain's humiliating defeat at the hands of the Americans in the Spanish-American War, and just as the Treaty of Paris was about to be signed stripping Spain of Cuba, Puerto Rico, and the Philippines, a writer who had urged Spain to abandon colonial exploits and look inward to restore her greatness was thrust upon the attention of the Spanish public.

Ganivet's attempt to shake Spain from her national illusions has proved more timely than Ganivet himself could have imagined. And his insistence that Spain's greatness has been misunderstood and undervalued, that it was in truth a greatness of spirit independent of the possession of territory or wealth must have been comforting to a nation incapable of prevailing against militarily stronger, materially wealthier and technologically more advanced powers.[12] Ganivet's stoical recommendation that Spain follow a course of dignified withdrawal seemed made to order as balm for injured national pride.[13]

Ganivet's fame and prestige were further confirmed by a celebration at the Madrid *Ateneo* in 1903 organized by his friends to commemorate the fifth anniversary of Ganivet's death. Participants included several of the Spanish intellectuals who were later to be numbered among the Generation of 1898: Unamuno, Martínez Ruiz (the future Azorín), and Ramiro de Maeztu.[14] Some twenty years later, the return of Ganivet's remains from Riga, first to Madrid and then to Granada in 1925, brought yet another outpouring of tributes to the man and his works, especially the *Idearium*.[15]

But these historic and commemorative moments were not alone responsible for the reputation of the *Idearium*. A continuous line of critical literature has kept the book alive for all those interested in Spanish culture. Much of this literature has been favorable. The book has been particularly praised for its penetration of the Spanish character and one hundred years after Ganivet's birth Melchor Fernández Almagro declared the *Idearium* to be an obligatory point of reference for all who attempt to delve into mysterious and unequivocal Spain.[16]

12 The book has also influenced the view of Spain taken by some foreign observers, most notably MAURICE LEGENDRE in *Portrait de L'Espagne* (1923) and WALDO FRANK in *Virgin Spain* (1926) who share Ganivet's perception of a virgin and individualistic land that has somehow strayed from her original course. GERALD BRENAN in his classic study of the roots of the Spanish civil war, *The Spanish Labyrinth* (Oxford, 1954), x-xii, offers almost exactly the same interpretation of the Spanish judicial sense as Ganivet.

13 RAMSDEN, *Angel Ganivet...*, 147-8, 147, n. 1, 148, n. 1, points out the element of «sour grapes» in this posture. MANUEL AZAÑA, «El *Idearium* de Angel Ganivet,» in *Obras completas* (México, 1966), I, 615-17 emphasizes that the consolation the work offered was a major reason for its success.

14 The twenty-year-old Ortega y Gasset also participated although his attitude toward the *Idearium* was quite guarded.

15 See RAMSDEN, *Angel Ganivet...*, 18-9, 22-4, for more details about the Athenaeum homage and these later ones, and the disputes which arose between Right and Left in 1925 around the figure of Ganivet on the occasion of the return of his remains to Spain.

16 See his notice on Ganivet in *El Libro Español,* VIII (1965), 129.

But alongside the favorable criticism another critical tradition has discerned many flaws in the *Idearium.* One of the earliest detractors was Miguel de Unamuno, whose *En torno al casticismo* now also holds an important place in the canon of works exploring Spanish problems and identity. The early friendship between Unamuno and Ganivet had lapsed since the two parted after the competitive exams in Greek in the spring of 1891. But after reading some of Ganivet's articles in *El Defensor* and the *Idearium,* in 1896 Unamuno initiated a correspondence which lasted until the consul's sucide. Part of this correspondence appeared in *El Defensor* from June to September of 1898 and was later published as *El porvenir de España* in 1912.[17] In this exchange of views about Spain and its future, Unamuno expresses a generally positive opinion of the *Idearium,* which he calls an «obra valiente» and one that stands out from the morass of contemporary Spanish literature.[18] But Unamuno also takes issue with a number of Ganivet's premises. He questions Ganivet's view of the Spanish colonial enterprise as one dedicated to spreading ideas and civilization rather than as a business venture. «¿Qué ideas?» asks Unamuno, denying that the Spaniards sought primarily to Christianize the New World instead of obtain gold and establish commercial monopolies there.[19] Still under the influence of socialism at this time, Unamuno faulted Ganivet for attributing too much authority to ideas in any case. Ideas, Unamuno says, are results, not causes; and changes in social organization occur in obedience to economic laws not as a result of politics or philosophy. Thus Unamuno declares that the establishment of the beet industry in Granada exercised more influence on the region than did the conquest by Ferdinand and Isabella, and the steel industry in the Basque country had more power to change people's lives than could an «army of ideologues» like Ganivet and himself.[20]

Several subsequent commentators have elaborated on Unamuno's sharpest criticisms of the *Idearium.* D. L. Shaw, José Antonio Maravall, and K. E. Shaw, for example, also fault Ganivet for failing to recognize the importance in Spanish life of economic and social forces.[21] Others

[17] GANIVET'S contribution appeared from 9 to 15 July, 1898 (see in *Obras,* II, 109-95) and from 6 to 14 September, 1898 (not in *Obras).* His July contribution, but not his September contribution, was included in *El porvenir de España.* An easily accessible complete text of the exchange, with an introduction by Unamuno, is MIGUEL DE UNAMUNO, *Obras completas* (New York, 1968), III, 638-95.

[18] UNAMUNO, *Obras,* III, 652. See also NICOLÁS MARÍA LÓPEZ's rather mixed early comments, «Ganivet y sus obras,» LÓPEZ's introduction to the first edition of *Cartas finlandesas,* Granada, 1898, 18-27.

[19] UNAMUNO, *Obras,* III, 641.

[20] *Ibid.,* 664. Unamuno was also one of many to comment on Ganivet's confusing the dogma of the Immaculate Conception with the virgin birth; see *ibid.,* 646 and 651 for Ganivet's assertion that he knew the difference but refused to make the clarification in the manuscript. See also in this context JAVIER HERRERO, «Spain as Virgin: Radical Traditionalism in Angel Ganivet,» *Homenaje a Juan López-Morillas,* José Amor y Vázquez and A. David Kossoff, eds. (Madrid: 1982), 247-56, for an excellent analysis of Ganivet's interpretation of the Virgin, and MATÍAS MONTES, «El dogma de la Inmaculada Concepción como interpretación de la mujer en la obra de Ganivet,» *Dusquesne Hispanic Review,* 13 (1968), 9-25.

[21] D. L. SHAW, *The Generation...,* 30; J. A. MARAVALL, «Ganivet y el tema

assail the book mainly for fabricating history and presenting a distorted version of Spanish culture to serve Ganivet's ideological purposes. Manuel Azaña dismisses the book as historically inaccurate, illogical, and misleading, treating as it does the entire range of Spanish culture as if everything could so nicely confirm Ganivet's interpretation. But, Azaña concludes, «plantearse a fondo los problemas pendientes en una de estas disciplinas, conocer siquiera los métodos, le habría bastado para no escribir el *Idearium.*»[22] Azaña finds «El crédito del *Idearium* es igual a la suma de cuanto sus lectores desconocen, multiplicada por la inhibición del juicio al leer.»[23]

Herbert Ramsden, whose *Angel Ganivet's 'Idearium español'* is the most thorough and severely critical study yet, also criticizes Ganivet's method, which he believes Ganivet derived largely from Taine, whose works the diplomat read in Antwerp. For Ramsden the book suffers from «an exaggerated emphasis on a simple, central, all-pervading 'idea,' with consequent attempts to justify that 'idea' by possibly unjustified selection from the boundless complexity of the civilization presented.»[24] Besides suffering from oversimplification and shallow determinism, the book is also marred by hopelessly ambiguous language and faulty logic.[25] «The *Idearium,*» Ramsden concludes, «is not a serious intellectual work; it is a work of intoxicated, therapeutic intellectualization.»[26] Yet Ramsden attributes the continued popularity of the work to some of its flaws: the ambiguity and illogic make it adaptable to diverse circumstances and readers.[27].

K. E. Shaw gives the work a similarly backhanded compliment. Discussing Ganivet's historical analysis and social theorizing he suggests that the merit of the *Idearium* lies rather in its creation of a myth whose function is to assuage the doubts and anxieties of a community that finds itself living amid conflicting values and purposes.[28] This reading probably comes closer to the secret of Ganivet's accomplishment than any other. Weak on fact, implausible in theory, the *Idearium* has satisfied generations of readers because it has given them cultural ideals, however Quixotic, to believe in.

de la autenticidad nacional,» *Revista de Occidente* 11 (1965), 389-409; K. E. SHAW, «Angel Ganivet: A Sociological Interpretation,» *Revista de Estudios Hispánicos,* II (1968), 181.

22 MANUEL AZAÑA, *Obras completas* (México, Oasis, 1966), I, 617-8.

23 *Ibid.* CÉSAR BARJA, *Libros y autores contemporáneos* (New York, 2nd ed., 1964), 16, agrees with Azaña. BARJA sees the *Idearium* as an ideological essay in which the author «más en realidad que interpretar la historia lo que Ganivet hace es intuirla, adivinarla y también aquí y allí, fantasearla.» He finds that any scrutiny of the political, social, and ideological principles behind the work, its historical suppositions and interpretations, and its conclusions will leave little that can be accepted and a great deal that must be rejected as arbitrary, chimerical and false.

24 *Angel Ganivet's...*, 155-6.

25 *Ibid.*, 163-4, 165-6, and 163 note 1; 182, n. 4; 188-9 for examples.

26 *Ibid.*, 150.

27 *Ibid.*, 89-90.

28 «Angel Ganivet...,» 180-81.

Nothing about the *Idearium* is more remarkable than its very optimism —«Yo tengo fe en el porvenir espiritual de España...» (I, 300) «... debemos confiar en el porvenir...» (I, 303). For in so much of his life and throughout his correspondence, Ganivet was consumingly pessimistic. This pessimism even cost him his life barely a year after his book's publication. Yet Ganivet had given a hint, in *Granada la bella,* of how pessimism and optimism can coexist in a single person. Referring to the novelist Alarcón and the poet Zorrilla, he says their works present an optimistic view of reality that contradicted their private beliefs. In a telling conjecture Ganivet guesses that the two would explain the contradiction by saying:

> Nuestras ideas son negativas y no sirven para el arte, que es cosa de crear, no de destruir; si escribimos con nuestras ideas, compondremos folletos de propaganda, no obras de arte. Y además, cuando pensamos, pensamos con nuestra cabeza, mientras que cuando creamos, creamos con todo nuestro ser y nos sale lo que está en nuestra sangre. Hay algo que está por encima de las fuerzas humanas. (I, 107)[29]

These lines suggest that Ganivet may have given the *Idearium* more optimism than his private thoughts allowed him in an attempt to create a positive work of art greater than the negative convictions that colored his view of existence. His success in doing this is indicated in part by the fact that of all the books of its genre written at the turn of the century, the *Idearium* has left the deepest mark on Spanish culture. Juan Marichal perhaps best conveyed the special place that Ganivet's analysis of Spain has had for many of his educated countrymen when he said of himself and others that reading the *granadino* is «una etapa genérica de las bibliografías intelectuales de incontables hombres de lengua castellana.»[30] During the Spanish Civil War, Marichal and his friends felt that both Ganivet and Mariano José de Larra were with them and that their writings were like the «últimos mensajes de hermanos mayores,» messages of consolation which «parecían ofrecernos la explicación de aquella terrible guerra, parecían advertirnos que los males españoles visibles eran a la vez antiguos y muy reparables.»[31] When Marichal left Europe in 1940 able to take only two or three books with him, one of them, he said, could not have failed to be Ganivet's *Idearium.*

Curiously, the *Idearium* originally saw the light of day without Ganivet's name attached. Only the dedication to «Francisco Ganivet Morcillo, «padre del autor» hints at the author. *Granada la bella* had also appeared anonymously, although the dedication to his mother similarly allowed a small group of friends to know the identity of its creator. Ganivet regarded

[29] Ganivet, an admirer of José María Pereda, may have found a line from Pereda's 1883 novel *Pedro Sánchez* also relevant to the optimism of the *Idearium:* «... hay mentiras necesarias y hasta indispensables, como son las del arte en cuanto tiende a embellecer la Naturaleza y dar mayor expansión y nobleza a los humanos sentimientos.»

[30] «Dos lecturas de Ganivet: 1937, 1965,» *Papeles de Son Armadans,* XL, 245.

[31] *Ibid.*

both these works as public property; they were written as part of his contribution to the spiritual welfare of Granada and Spain as a whole, and not for personal profit. Ganivet believed that writers should be generous with their ideas so that their thoughts could benefit others. In the *Idearium* Ganivet states that the concept of intellectual property is based on a profound error. If a person's labors are motivated by the idea of gain, then it is appropriate for the reward to be a monetary one, but this principle should not apply to works of art or science, «las cuales no deben tener otro motivo de inspiración que el amor a la verdad o la belleza» (I, 250).

The key to understanding his reason for publishing these two works anonymously can be found in the *Idearium* itself, where Ganivet puts forth his conception of the communal origins of cultural products. Ganivet viewed his own individual works as rooted in and nourished by a larger, organic artistic tradition:

> Yo no he aceptado nunca como cosa legítima la propiedad intelectual, hasta tengo mis dudas acerca de la propiedad de las ideas. El fruto nace de la flor; pero no es de la flor, es del árbol. El hombre es como una eflorescencia de la especie y sus ideas no son suyas, sino de la especie que las nutre y las conserva. (I, 249)

«*Cartas finlandesas*»

In response to requests from some friends in Granada curious about life in exotic Finland, late in 1896 Ganivet began the twenty-two brief essays that comprise his *Cartas finlandesas*.[32] This is an engaging potpourri of facts and impressions drawn from Ganivet's Nordic days and intended to disclose the spirit of the country in descriptions of Finnish government, architecture, amusements, cuisine, and death rituals. And like Ganivet's other observations of foreign cultures, the *Cartas* are sprinkled with references to Spain and his observations suggest critical reflections on her culture —recalling José Cadalso's *Cartas marruecas*.[33] The *Cartas* also recall Ganivet's private correspondence with Navarro Ledesma about Belgium in their comments on an alien culture and people. But contrary to his disdain for the Belgians, Ganivet appears to have liked and respected the Finns, although he chides them, as he did practically everyone, for pursuing materialistic interests.

In comparing the Finns to the Spaniards, Ganivet frequently finds the Finns superior. He discovers, for instance, that the Finns know considerably more about Spain and the rest of the world than the Spaniards

[32] The first twenty letters were published in *El Defensor* from 14 October 1896 to 9 July 1897. Letters 21 and 22 appeared there on April 20 and 26. All twenty-two letters appeared in book form in September, 1898.

[33] See JUAN ROS GARCÍA, «Los caminos del ensayo: Ganivet y las *Cartas finlandesas,*» *Estudios literarios dedicados al Profesor Mariano Baquero Goyanes,* Murcia, 1974, 452-4, and MATÍAS MONTES HUIDOBRO'S «*Cartas finlandesas:* Ganivet, agonista de la percepción y del lenguaje,» *Revista de Estudios Hispánicos,* X (1976), 3-30.

know about any place but Spain, which gives Ganivet an opportunity to criticize his compatriots for their insularity and petty, parochial mentality. He suggests a remedy for these defects in the emulation of Finnish practicality; this is another example of the «hispanization» of foreign practices that Ganivet recommended in the *Idearium.* One such beneficial practical reform would be, Ganivet said, to follow the Finnish example and open up the universities to a broad public and give them a greater role in the nation's cultural life. The universities should, therefore, incorporate the fine arts (although Ganivet shrank from proposing incorporation of the engineering academy, despite the good results of this he had observed in Belgium) and sponsor both artistic and scientific programs open to the public, since they could thereby achieve both greater influence and financial independence.

As in *Granada la bella* and *La conquista* Ganivet devotes considerable attention in *Cartas finlandesas* to women and their place in society. Although he found Finnish women better educated and more competent in worldly matters than their Spanish counterparts, and he numbered several accomplished women among his friends in Helsinki, he nevertheless conceded to his readers that he preferred the Spanish style «familia sentimental» to the Finnish style «familia intelectual.»[34] He even asserts in Letter VIII that «la idea constitutiva de la naturaleza de la mujer es la de rendirse y someterse, de mejor o peor gana, a la autoridad natural del hombre» (I, 731). And although he approved of a woman undertaking studies that would not interfere with her domestic functions, she should not study with an eye toward emancipation, or better that she never leave the kitchen (I, 733).[35] In general the *granadino* sensed a lack of passion between the sexes in Finland and this was not to his liking. But he admired the Finn's open-mindedness toward divorce —a shocking and forbidden concept in nineteenth-century Roman Catholic Spain— and the ability of former spouses to remain friends despite the remarriage of one to a lover (I, 737).

Several of the *Cartas* dwell on Finnish literature, foreshadowing Ganivet's studies of Scandinavian authors, *Hombres del norte,* written in 1897 and 1898. One of the longest of these, XX (18 pages in the *Obras completas*), is devoted to the Finnish national epic, the *Kalevala*,[36] «una creación étnica y territorial» which Ganivet judged to be among the world's best epics. Comparing it to the *Iliad* for the purpose of identifying its distinctly Finnish qualities, Ganivet stresses again the Finn's attenuated passion. There is not a scene that a Spaniard would recognize as a love scene, he says; the only love that wins the homage of the heroes and the enthusiasm of the poet is maternal love. The motives for action

34 Nicolás María López, «Ganivet y sus obras,» the introduction to the first edition of *Cartas,* 13, states that the information about Finnish women was what most surprised *granadinos* and elicited the most comment.

35 See also I, 733, 742, 756. See Geraldine M. Scanlon, *La polémica feminista en la España contemporánea: 1868-1974* (Madrid, 1976), for background on the issues of women's emancipation in Spain in Ganivet's time.

36 An English translation is by Francis Peabody Magoun, Jr., *The Kalevala: Or Poems of the Kaleva District,* edited by Elias Lönnrot (Harvard, 1963).

are also less than Ganivet would have them be: few ideals and many material necessities, namely those associated with the harsh northern climate. But despite its psychological deficiencies, Ganivet praises the *Kalevala* for its true and sincere humanity which warrants its presentation to the Spanish people as a little known and notable foreign literary monument.

Ganivet's pioneering efforts to educate and inform his countrymen about the cultures of other nations give both *Cartas finlandesas* and *Hombres del norte* an enduring historical importance. Ortega y Gasset referred to these works as «grandes libros europeos» and named Ganivet, along with Unamuno, as the first Spaniards to have truly penetrated the culture of northern and central Europe and to have thereby made «universal el horizonte de la cultura española.»[37]

As the summer of 1897 approached, Ganivet obtained another leave and headed for Spain. When he returned to Granada in mid-June he was a local celebrity; not only was his position of Spanish consul in Helsinki an impressive one, but he had also recently published, *La conquista,* in March of 1897, and the *Idearium* would appear in August.

[37] Prologue to Ganivet, *Cartas finlandesas y hombres del norte* (Espasa Calpe, 1961) 5th edition, xii-xiv.

Chapter 4

A SUMMER IN SPAIN

The summer of 1897 was Ganivet's last in Spain, and it was enormously productive. He wrote, solidified old friendships, made new ones, and aroused the artistic and intellectual aspirations of his contemporaries in Granada.

Ganivet arrived in Granada in the middle of June, and in early July the *Cofradía del Avellano,* a group of Granada's restless artists and literati, offered a banquet in his honor. This intellectual brotherhood had been coalescing for several years, but it was Ganivet who now emerged as its leader and gave it a center and a direction. The group, many of whose members appear thinly disguised in *Los trabajos del infatigable creador, Pío Cid,* was an elite one, comprised of both older and younger writers, together with several artists, all of whom were concerned about the state of literature and art in Granada. Hostile to the supposed modernization of their city, the *Cofradía* would assemble for discussion in a downtown cafe and stroll up to the Fuente del Avellano, one of the picturesque, unspoiled fountains on the outskirts of Granada where the *tertulia* would begin. Nicolás María López described Ganivet's participation in the group's informal *tertulias* in the following terms:

> Al tomar Ganivet la palabra, todos callábamos. Su voz era dulce y suave, a veces rápida y cortada, a ratos pausada y solemne. Hablaba de países o ciudades lejanas; exponía el asunto de un libro; hacía la crítica de una obra dramática, moderna o clásica, o trazaba, en cuatro rasgos, la semblanza de los grandes escritores... (NML, 18-19).

The idealism and critical spirit of the group were typical of the Generation of '98; the fruit of their gatherings was their publication of the *Libro de Granada,* conceived that summer and published in 1899, several months after Ganivet's death. A book of stories, poems, and sketches about the city, it included eight pieces by Ganivet as well as a prologue he hastily prepared while still in Granada; in the latter, Ganivet voices the hope that other collaborative efforts by the city's illustrious authors would follow and would one day collectively form a résumé of the city's intellectual life. Indeed, what Ganivet seems to have had in mind was a small renaissance of culture and art in his native city in imitation of the Greek city-states he so admired.

«Libro de Granada»

In *Granada la bella,* Ganivet had urged the citizens of his native city to improve local culture through their own spiritual creations. In the *Libro de Granada,* he took a more active role in promoting this end. The book consists of eight chapters—each named for a representative feature of Granada—the Alhambra, the Avellano fountain, the Albaicín district, etc. and containing one story, sketch or poem by each of the four authors Ganivet, Nicolás María López, Gabriel Ruiz de Almodóvar, and Matías Méndez Vellido. Some of the works had been read aloud at the *Cofradía*'s meetings, and it was at one of the last of these that the decision was made to publish a book. It was an idealistic venture, since in Granada publishing literature was a costly undertaking. Ganivet supplied much of the impetus for the project and his collaborators much regretted that Ganivet did not live to see the publication, blaming their «maldita pereza» and tardiness in completing their assignments as well as delays on the part of the publisher (LSLP, 32; NML, 20). However, four of eight pieces were published during Ganivet's lifetime in *El Defensor* in July of 1897.[1]

The eight pieces written for *El libro de Granada* represent a variety of genres and themes that were to be developed more fully in subsequent writings by the author, particularly in his play, *El escultor de su alma.* These pieces, three poems —«El rey de la Alhambra,» «Un bautizo,» and «Los grajos,»— and five prose sketches, «Una derrota de los greñudos,» «Trogloditas,» «El alma de las calles,» «Las ruinas de Granada,» and «De mi novia la que murió,»[2] are unified by a critique of the present, a sense of loss and nostalgia for the past, and a preoccupation with the nature of art. In keeping with his didactic commitment, Ganivet seeks to infuse the city of Granada with a mystical significance that is to serve as inspiration for its citizens, especially its artists. Granada is the symbol of a lost wholeness that must be recreated by looking toward the past and by incorporating its richness into the future. In «El rey de la Alhambra,» a *romance,* a father, in answer to his son's questions, explains that the man they see near the Alhambra's *Puerta de la Justicia* is a dumb and blind beggar who cannot even cry about his misfortunes because his eyes have been completely destroyed. In the second stanza the boy asks his father for a coin and gives it to the beggar, who kisses it and hides it is his ragged clothing. The poet calls the beggar an «estatua del infortunio» and an «imagen de la injusticia de este mundo» (II, 694). At

[1] These appeared as follows: «El rey de la Alhambra,» July 7; «Los grajos,» July 13; «Trogloditas,» July 21; and «El alma de las calles,» July 27. See LSLP, 32-3. HERRERO in JH, 133, offers a penetrating study of Ganivet's poetry and contends that the poems in *Libro de Granada* were written when the author felt the inspiration and were later inserted into the prose works: «... poesías escritas en los años 1892 a 1893 se incluyen en composiciones de 1897.»

[2] Additional poems are incorporated in «Las ruinas de Granada» and «De mi novia la que murió.»

nightfall the beggar takes refuge in a crevice of a crumbling wall near the Alcázar. And in the last stanza, as the boy and his father continue on their way, the sight of four gravediggers carrying a coffin inspires the child to ask what would happen to the beggar if his death went unnoticed. The father replies that the body would turn to dust and an Alcázar would be his tomb; thus the beggar, who was the king of sorrow, will, in the end, have a royal mausoleum. This is the earliest version of the figure of Juanico el Ciego, also a beggar, who appears in *Los trabajos* and who commits suicide by jumping from one of the towers of the Alhambra. It also prefigures Pedro Mártir of *El escultor de su alma,* who dies and is inmortalized in stone beneath the Alhambra. Here we find the first of several associations that Ganivet makes between death and the Alhambra, and it is worthy of special note since previously in his work symbols of Spain are seen as engendering creative forces, not as their grave.

«Trogloditas,» a meditative essay, is part of the chapter «En el Sacro Monte.»[3] In this piece the first person narrator invites his companion, a paleontologist, to investigate some contemporary pre-history. Here, in the whitewashed caves, the narrator says, primitive man still lives, although instead of hunting he has learned to live together in a family with his domestic animals (a child whose eye was pecked out by a turkey appears, and her presence indicates a bitter consequence of this way of life). These troglodytes have a limited conception of reality, which they, like Plato's cavedwellers, see reflected on the walls of their cave. When they leave the dark cave they are overwhelmed by the spectacle of light and nature and must hastily return to their cavern. The troglodytes are like the Spaniards, who began as moles and after many centuries still behave like them, both in the caves and in much more elevated positions. So, despite the good-natured tone of the story, the criticism of Spanish insularity and obscurantism it contains is fierce.

«El espíritu de las calles» looks toward the national artistic tradition and recalls *Granada la bella* in its assertion that art and the spirit of individual streets powerfully influence the soul of a locality and its inhabitants. A superior artist, the author explains, allows the *alma* of a specific area and of its works of art to infuse his own work, rendering it greater than what any one man, even a genius, could create by himself. This same notion of a geographic centering for the creative act necessitates in *El escultor,* that Pedro Mártir return to Granada since it is only within the confines of his own culture that the artist is able to connect with his creative forces. It would seem, therefore, that for Ganivet the artist never speaks solely with an individual voice but is the vessel through which the *Volksgeist* is transmitted. Here Ganivet again recalls Bécquer, who conceived the relation between the poet and his poetry in quite similar terms: «Podrá no haber poetas; pero siempre / habrá poesía.»[4]

[3] JH, 107-11, gives a particularly interesting reading of this section.
[4] BÉCQUER, *Rimas,* José Luis Cano, ed. (Salamanca, 1965), 25.

Bécquer, indeed, is a more significant presence in Ganivet's *ars poetica,* especially as expressed in the pieces written for *Libro de Granada,* than has yet been noted. Just as Bécquer's *Leyendas* were born from sites heavy with tradition so, too, does Ganivet find that the tradition transmitted from generation to generation through fountains, plazas, streets, and ruins seems to vibrate with sleeping voices that only speak to the poet: «Muchas cosas más dicen las calles. Ellas mismas declaran lo que quieren ser y sugieren a veces ideas nuevas y proyectos útiles» (II, 700).

Another of these pieces, «Las ruinas de Granada,» is an unusual essay that looks toward the past, i.e., the present, from the perspective of the future, thirty centuries from now. Written in the form of a dialogue Ganivet presents a poet and a wise man on a visit to the ruins of what had once been Granada. Subtitled «Ensueño,» this sketch resembles science fiction in its use of inventions —*aerostatos* that carry passengers across the sky and the *ideófono,* an ebony box that sings when activated by its owner's eyes and thoughts.

The dialogue of the poet and the wise man represents the *desdoblamiento* of the author: the creative self and the contemplative self. The difference between the two depicts two possible ways of perceiving the world. For the wise man there is no difference between the human artist who captures the essence of life in a work of art and the volcano that petrifies a city in a given moment of time as if it were «un escultor iluminado por la Providencia» (II, 704). The poet rejects the wise man's «visión de arqueólogo» and offers a landscape that contains the ideal, one that surpasses the human and yet is born from it. The poet seeks to find within the ruins «los restos miserables de las cosas que fueron y ya no son... Si hay algo más hermoso que la vida es el amargor y el desencanto que deja tras sí la existencia» (II, 703). Thus does memory hover over life, more poignant and yet somehow truer to life than life itself. The ruins offer the poet the possibility of reconstructing the universal from the particular, of selecting a fragment of human memory that can become eternal as a work of art.

The wise man, however, falsely ignores the selective element intrinsic to the artistic imagination and believes that a truthful vision can be achieved only from a frozen moment of life such as that offered in a Pompeii-like scene. Science, Ganivet would seem to say, which seeks truth in the global, indiscriminant specimen, loses the superior truth that art can render.

The sketch ends on a pessimistic note as the *ideófono* sadly sings «La canción de la piedra,» whose closing stanza says: «Si muerte y vida son sueño / si todo en el mundo sueña / yo doy mi vida de hombre / por soñar muerto, en la piedra» (II, 711). Life is to be understood, therefore, by a process of recollection, a turning back into the ruins of our past and, from the fragments found, create a work of art that outlives us and that dreams us. The stone's dream is the poetic activity through which life is to be viewed and judged. The contemplative self, personified by the wise man, must give way to the creative self, the artist who in his *ensueño* invents life and thereby overcomes death. This theme will be made more explicit in *El escultor de su alma.* The relationship between these two pieces is further indicated by the inclusion of the two poems, «¡Qué silenciosos dormís!» and «La canción de la piedra» in both.

In early August Ganivet left Granada with his brother Francisco and his sisters Josefa and Isabel. They travelled to Madrid where Francisco was to continue his studies and where the author of the *Idearium* attended the funeral, on August 13, of the Prime Minister Cánovas del Castillo, who had been assassinated a few days earlier. Then the consul and his sisters went on to Barcelona where Ganivet, apparently without previous explanations, introduced his sisters to Amelia Roldán and his son Angel Tristán. The following Monday Ganivet organized a group excursion to the nearby resort of Sitges, where he remained for several weeks while his sisters, Amelia, and little Angel returned to Barcelona after a few days.

In Sitges, Ganivet established ties with the *Cau Ferrat,* an active group of Catalonian artists, including Santiago Rusiñol and Miguel Utrillo, who were in the forefront of Spanish modernism. Although Ganivet wrote in praise of the *Cau* in a chronicle in *El Defensor* describing the group and praising some of its activities, in particular the erection of a statute in honor of El Greco and a production of Maeterlinck's *L'Intruse,* he apparently made a poor impression on Utrillo, who later described him as an «anormal» who continually engaged in violent arguments, particularly about political or artistic matters: «Se ponía frenético, pálido, desencajado, babeaba y cuando la cosa se ponía tan grave que debía terminarse lógicamente por vías de hecho, se levantaba del asiento y se marchaba. Así casi todos los días.»[5]

Despite this, in early September Ganivet wrote enthusiastically to both Francisco Seco Lucena and Nicolás María López about his experiences with the Catalonians, whom he judged the most active artistic group in Spain and who had obvious affinities with the *Cofradía del Avellano* in Granada (NML, 81-2; LSLP, 94-5). Ganivet began promoting relations between the two groups. He gave Rusiñol a letter of introduction to the *Cofradía,* and Rusiñol offered to send some of his works for their next exhibit in Granada. Further, Ganivet's desire to broaden the narrow perspectives of Spanish provincial life with news of the world beyond its borders and to participate in Catalonia's cultural activity led him, in response to an invitation to contribute to the prestigious Barcelona newspaper *La Vanguardia,* to give his permission to reprint whatever the paper chose from *El Defensor.*

Had Ganivet remained longer in Spain he might well have taken a leading role in stirring new intellectual and artistic activities and alliances among this generation just beginning to be heard. But Ganivet's professional responsibilities called him away again and in late September, 1897, the consul returned to Helsinki along with his sisters, Amelia, and his son.

[5] Quoted in RAMSDEN, *Angel Ganivet's...*, 144.

Chapter 5

HELSINKI AGAIN

By early fall of 1897 Ganivet was back in Helsinki with his family, his sisters Josefa and Isabel, Amelia Roldán and Angel Tristán, and he found his domestic life a pleasant one as he began what he called his «segunda campaña en Helsinfors» (LSLP, 97). In mid-October he wrote to López that his sisters were happy in Finland and that he was teaching them French: «Cada día resulta mejor para todos la solución que yo di a los asuntos domésticos» (NML, 87).

He resumed his writing at a hectic pace and in letters to friends discussed his literary projects for the next two years —in 1899 *at the latest* he planned another long visit to Spain— and he encouraged them to finish their books: «mi deseo es que todos sacudáis la modorra, y que por lo menos los cuatro que nos hemos reunido literariamente, y nos hemos echado a la calle en el non-nato *Libro de Granada,* dejemos bien puesto nuestro nombre» (NML, 84). In this statement we can see both the importance that finishing a work had for Ganivet as well as his recognition of the *granadino* laziness, though, as his own example showed, it could be overcome. Yet finishing a work did not insure satisfaction with it. In the same letter Ganivet stresses the importance of an appropriate point of view in a literary work and admits: «no sé aún cuál es mi verdadero punto de vista, y por esto no he podido hacer aún nada que me deje satisfecho, en cuanto es posible quedar satisfecho de la propia obra» (NML, 86).

«*Los trabajos del infatigable creador, Pío Cid*»

The scope of Ganivet's creative and critical activities had by now enlarged considerably. His first task was a series of essays on Scandinavian literature, *Hombres del norte,* which occupied him from November, 1897, until his death. On December 1, he started a new, philosophical novel, *Los trabajos del infatigable creador, Pío Cid* (henceforth referred to as *Los trabajos),* a sequel to *La conquista* which Ganivet had considered «como prólogo o preparación espiritual para *Los trabajos*» and part of a larger cycle of projected works (NML, 92, 95). «La idea fundamental» he told López, «es la transformación social y humana por medio de inventos, lo mismo que en *La conquista,* sólo que ahora la nación es

España, y los inventos son originales, como verás» (NML, 95-6). He was also aware of a relationship between *Los trabajos* and the *Idearium;* while in the midst of writing *Los trabajos,* he commented to a friend that in this work «verá usted hecho hombre el hispano-semita que se esconde en el *Idearium*» (LSLP, 121).[1]

Originally, Ganivet had envisioned that the novel would consist of 12 «*trabajos*» or chapters, like the labors of Hercules, but at the time of his death he had written and published only six. He believed these six, however, to possess a unity of their own sufficient to stand as an independent work until he finished the remaining chapters (NML, 97). In a letter to López, Ganivet insisted that he had the second six chapters thought out, although not written, and that when completed they would perfectly round out the work (NML, 101-2).[2]

Ganivet had apparently conceived of *Los trabajos* a good deal before he wrote the account of his protagonist's adventures in Spain, which helps to explain the rapidity with which he produced the story. Devoting December and January, a time when his consular duties were minimal, to this project, he completed five chapters of almost five hundred pages by January 31, 1898. The enormous energy expended in this remarkable endeavor left him exhausted but proud and necessitated a short period of recuperation before completion of the sixth trabajo of 75 pages.

The six *trabajos* («Pío Cid intenta desasnar a unos estudiantes,» «Pío Cid pretende gobernar a unas amazonas,» «Pío Cid quiere formar un buen poeta,» «Pío Cid emprende la reforma política de España,» «Pío Cid acude a levantar a una mujer caída,» «Pío Cid asiste a una enferma de frivolidad») chronicle Pío Cid's life in Spain upon his return from his African adventures. As the story begins, an old Pío Cid is living an obscure, abstinent, solitary and eccentric existence in a Madrid boarding house, in an atmosphere reminiscent of Galdós' depictions of the Spanish capital. His parents, sister, and niece are all dead, and he has been rejected as a suitor by a woman horrified by the written account of his African exploits, presumably *La conquista.* During the course of the novel Pío Cid teaches the illiterate maid Purilla to read and write, helps change the vocation of Adolfo de la Gandaria and his sister Consuelo, falls in love, and assumes the financial burdens of his beloved Martina's family of six women (nine months later he becomes the father of twins). He also acts as a matchmaker, although he himself adamantly refuses to marry. In the middle of the work Pío Cid briefly emerges from his life of obscurity to enter politics, withdrawing mysteriously after being elected *diputado* in his native district of provincial Granada. He composes and reads to his Granadan friends his philosophy of life, which he entitles *Ecce homo,* and he tantalizes them with its abrupt ending.

[1] A. A. PARKER in a recent article has emphasized that both *La conquista* and *Los trabajos* «should be read as a commentary on the *Idearium...*» «The novels of Ganivet,» *Homenaje a Juan López-Morillas* (Madrid, 1982), 370.

[2] See GM: ET, 46-7, for the chapter titles and brief outline of the unfinished portion. The completed section of *Los trabajos* was originally published in two volumes due to Ganivet's «horror» of large books. See NML, 69.

He promises more, in the form of a tragedy, to be revealed upon his death, and he prophesies that his friends will not have to wait long for this event.

Returning to Madrid, Pío Cid provides the beautiful but ill-fated orphan Mercedes a temporary home and he teaches the world-weary Duchess of Almadura about love and her young son about agriculture and the interrelatedness of human endeavors. As the finished portion of the novel ends, Pío Cid leaves Madrid to begin a new life in Barcelona. In Ganivet's outline of the unifinished six chapters, published by Gallego Morell (GM: ET, 46-7), Pío Cid reinvigorates the Spanish theatre, and, after a number of other adventures, he dies.

The tone of this novel is elegiac. Angel, the narrator, like Pío Cid a *granadino* residing in Madrid, wishes to record for posterity the deeds of his «amado héroe» who is also described as «casi un santo.» Angel, through his contact with Pío Cid, has been transformed from an ambitious young man into a contemplative philosopher. He resembles Unamuno's Angela Carballino, the narrator of *San Manuel Bueno, mártir,* in that both posthumously record the life of a «saint,» a man who himself lacks faith yet inspires it in others; both narrators have been spiritually and philosophically influenced by their subject and the position of both narrators as witnesses consciously affirms the veracity of the text.

The identification of the narrator with Ganivet in name and place of origin suggests an autobiographical connection which Herrero and Agudiez in particular have discussed and documented; however, it is Pío Cid himself who serves to express in the novel the author's world view and experience.[3]

In *Los trabajos* we see a reelaboration and summing up of the major themes Ganivet had explored in earlier writings: pedagogy and education; Spain and her destiny; the Spanish character and its need to cultivate the qualities of charity, sacrifice, and spirituality; a philosophical concern for existential problems; a struggle with skepticism; the conflict between the desires on the one hand for a contemplative life and on the other for an active formative influence in the world; the importance of the formation of a family; his vision of women; and a reworking of the classic Spanish theme of honor. Of particular interest to us in this chapter is Ganivet's concern with the relation between artistic creation and love in its various forms, and with the moral dimension of art.

These themes are all developed through elements drawn from the classical world, most notable in the title, the Christian tradition, and the literary and military heroes of Spain. Hercules, Jesus, el Cid and Don Quixote are all present in Pío Cid as Ganivet reworks traditional artistic,

[3] See HERRERO, «El elemento biográfico en *Los trabajos del infatigable creador, Pío Cid,*» *Hispanic Review,* XXXIV, 95-110, and AGUDIEZ, *Las novelas...*, 132-48. AZORÍN, in his 1904 «La psicología de Pío Cid» in *Obras selectas* (Madrid, 1953), 1054-5 writes of «uno de estos españoles representativos: de Angel Ganivet, o lo que es igual, de su héroe —Pío Cid—, tal como queda retratado en *Los trabajos.*»

cultural, and religious themes and figures. His hero seeks not to conquer but to transform those around him, and he succeeds in doing so.

Los trabajos, with its paucity of plot, dramatic conflict, characterization (with the exception of Pío Cid who dominates the narrative), and descriptions, and with its enormous reliance on dialogue, breaks, as did *La conquista,* with many of the conventions of the Spanish novel of the late nineteenth century. Ganivet's analysis of Laurence Sterne's narrative technique actually describes Ganivet's technique in *Los trabajos.* He comments on Sterne's minimal use of plot, «como un hilo tejido por una araña, roto a cada momento por el choque de las digresiones y reanudado sobre las digresiones mismas» (NML, 51). This «debilidad de acción» represented aesthetic progress for Ganivet, with the consequence that the «melodrama y la novela de acción brutal y complicada... quedarán... relegados para el uso de los salvajes de Europa.» Nowadays, he declares, the great contemporary writers are psychologists who «eligen acciones breves en las que... ocurren transformaciones íntimas» (NML, 51-2).

The dramatic core of each of the *trabajos* is a «transformación íntima» in Pío Cid and in those with whom he comes in contact. The digressions that characterize *Los trabajos* (like the intercalated tales in *Don Quixote)* lend a spiderweb quality to the narration by commenting on events in the text («Elección de esposa de Abd-el-Malik» II, 159-167), providing literary criticism and an additional point of view to the narrative («Protoplasma,» II, 656-77), and shaping the narrative through the introduction of characters who, in Cervantine fashion, transcend their roles in the inserted tale and assume active roles in the «main» text («Juanico el ciego,» II, 405-24).[4] Passages of poetry inserted into the text also supply commentary on the action («El cazador herido,» II, 254), a vehicle for literary criticism («Serenata,» II, 239), and a means of expressing the extraordinary reaction to an experience («Hija de Oriente,» II, 376-7).[5]

Purilla, the illiterate maid, is the first to be transformed by Pío Cid. Pío Cid's lessons here exemplify his selfless pedagogical vocation, one shared by his creator, and his radical view of education as best provided by teachers independent of official institutions who give students individual instruction and serve as a goad «que les arranque de su miserable rutina espiritual» (II, 38).[6] Purilla is an emblematic figure. At times, when teaching Purilla, Pío Cid has the sensation that it is not a poor servant at his bedside «sino España, toda España, que viene a leer, escribir y pensar...» (II, 43). What Pío Cid attempts to do with her may be seen as a concrete example of what he proposed for his country in the *Idearium.* He encourages Purilla to improve herself and to ennoble her profession, but he warns her not to attempt to become something other

[4] Francisco García Lorca, *Angel Ganivet...*, 38-9, discusses some other Cervantine traits of *Los trabajos.* Gonzalo Sobejano, *Nietzsche en España* (Madrid, 1967), 273, also indicates several Cervantine episodes.

[5] JH, 171-4, offers an important interpretation of this poem.

[6] See also II, 361-4 and II, 516-19, where Pío Cid expresses the same beliefs and in the latter case, acts on them.

than what she is. Similarly, he had urged Spain to improve itself internally by discovering and enhancing its true nature and not being led astray by a desire to imitate other nations and to seek to become something it is not. To Purilla, Pío Cid offers the possibility of a fortunate marriage as a reward for her efforts, to Spain, Ganivet offers the promise of a renewed sense of purpose and spiritual leadership of the Hispanic world —but in neither case are the benefits material.

Purilla's significance as an example of spiritual growth or intimate transformation becomes the greater when she decides to become a hospital nun. Pío Cid explains that her inspiration for self-improvement was inspired by her unrequited love for a man, and now she can share that love with all people, especially the most wretched. (Herrero has pointed to the parallel between the transformation of both Purilla's and Ganivet's frustrated love for an individual into a general and unlimited love for mankind that stood as the obverse of his often expressed misanthropy [JH, 42].)

Pío Cid, too, undergoes an interior transformation due to love in the first *trabajo* when, at the students' urging, he attends a masked ball where he meets a young masked woman with whom he falls in love (on the spot, before he even learns her name) and with whom he decides that very evening to spend the rest of his life. Pío Cid had previously claimed to have given up love in favor of something greater but the rebirth of this emotion is so moving that he is overwhelmed by sadness and tears, which the young woman tenderly kisses away in the most moving moment of the novel.[7]

One of the results of the union of Martina Gomara, the masked woman, and Pío Cid is the conscious violation of the Spanish bourgeois conventions of courtship and marriage. Pío Cid, who has immediately assumed the role of *de facto* although adamantly not *de jure* husband, holds that the creation in twenty-four hours of this «natural» family, flying in the face of society's artificial laws and customs, is a testimony to the power of love (II, 265). Subsequently, however, he is instrumental in arranging the marriage of Martina's cousin Paca and fostering the probable engagement of her cousin Valentina (and in Granada, unbeknownst to Martina, his intervention and generosity pave the way for a marriage there), which prompts Martina's resentment at this apparent contradiction. Why should her cousins marry and not she? Further, she is resentful that Pío Cid has a man's privilege to flaunt convention while a woman in identical circumstances is shunned.

Pío Cid assures Martina that she is «su mujer» and urges her to pay no heed to society, and to attempt to be less possessive in her love.

Ganivet views traditional marriage as an emotional straightjacket that virtually imposes fidelity on a couple, regardless of the course their feelings may take. In a country where divorce did not exist, a free union, such as Pío Cid's with Martina (or Ganivet's with Amelia), offered an option for terminating a relationship.

[7] See SOBEJANO, «Ganivet...,» 139 for a fine analysis of this scene.

Pío Cid's influence on Adolfo de la Gandaria, a State Department Attaché in the third *trabajo,* is another example of a «transformación íntima.» Pío Cid perceives a poetic temperament in Gandaria, and under the master's guidance the wealthy young man abandons his diplomatic career, a career which Pío Cid insists is a waste of time given Spain's wretched situation. Pío Cid's insistence that his nation must recover lost spiritual vigor and be content with the modest role it plays in world affairs again recalls the *Idearium.* By encouraging his young friend to change his direction, Ganivet seems to be reiterating that the only way Spain can regain its spiritual vigor is by turning its creative energies inward instead of pursuing unrealistic or misguided external goals.

Pío Cid does have faith and hope in the future of his country, but like other characters in novels by members of the Generation of '98 (and their creators, especially Baroja), Pío Cid has little faith in Spain's parliamentary government. He accurately predicts that it will not last a full century and that the appropriate government for Spain is a «gobierno fuerte y duro, como nuestro temperamento» (II, 201). Near the end of the novel the same idea reappears when Pío Cid discounts the possibility of a republic taking root on Spanish soil, because the Spaniards lack the necessary habits of order and regularity to govern themselves and thus need a dictator and artillery at every intersection to impose discipline —a foreshadowing of Joaquín Costa's famous call for a «cirujano de hierro.»[8]

In the course of the novel, Gandaria's poetic vocation grows, further demonstrating the acuity of Pío Cid's human judgments, and the occasions when he presents his master with his poetic efforts give Pío Cid the opportunity to voice his opinions (here again a «portavoz» for Ganivet's own on poetry and literary criticism). The best critic, he tells Gandaria, is an unbiased and disinterested friend who sees the work with love and who, without any desire to display his own wit, will impartially point out the weaknesses he sees. «Aspira a ser poeta,» he tells Gandaria, «aunque la crítica le maltrate, y a ser un gran poeta, aunque el público le insulte...» (II, 247).[9]

Pío Cid's lessons to Gandaria, like those of his creator to his *cofra-*

[8] A selection of JOAQUÍN COSTA's most important work is available in Rafael Pérez de la Dehesa's edition, *Oligarquía y caciquismo, colectivismo agrario y otros escritos* (Madrid: Alianza Editorial, 3d ed., 1973). For more information on Costa and the Generation of 1898 see PÉREZ DE LA DEHESA, *El pensamiento de Costa y su influencia en el 98* (Madrid: Sociedad de Estudios y Publicaciones, 1966). Pío Baroja's Manuel Alcázar who longed in *Aurora roja* for an «hombre fuerte» comes to mind here.

[9] Like Gandaria, Ganivet found his literary vocation waxing and his diplomatic one waning. In mid-January of 1898, as he was probably finishing this section of *Los trabajos,* he wrote to his friend Rafael Gago that; «aunque supiera que un sólo español había de leer lo que escribo, seguiría escribiendo, puesto que me ha dado por ahí y con la pluma me distraigo más que con ninguna otra cosa» (LSLP, 121-2). The growing sense of himself as a writer who meets just his

des, about the importance of literary creation and the value of unprejudiced literary criticism are complemented by «practical» examples. (Ganivet sent his own creations to Granada to stimulate and encourage his friends.) Pío Cid, explaining to Gandaria that the most important element in poetry is the «motivo poético,» an impression that produces a profound intellectual and sentimental germination, picks a motif from his large store and as a demonstration writes a poem based on it for his pupil. But this master/disciple exchange is not so straightforward as it first appears. It actually works on two levels; the literary lesson contains a moral lesson as well. On the surface Pío Cid and Gandaria talk about writing poetry. Underlying this subject, in the content of Gandaria's verses and Pío Cid's responses, is a dialogue on Gandaria's unsuccessful attempt to win Martina's favor. Pío Cid, knowing that Gandaria's efforts are in vain, gently informs the lovesick young man through the critique of his poetry and the «demonstration poems» that he is making a fool of himself. In a traditional novel a «husband» could be expected to react quite differently to Gandaria's behavior, which could be interpreted as an affront to his honor. Pío Cid follows neither literary nor moral conventions; thus the friendship between the two is preserved without

material necessities through his diplomatic employment is also evident in his letter of April 16, 1898 to López:

> Satisfechas las necesidades apremiantes de la tripa, dedícate a trabajar en cosas de tu gusto, con lo que te distraerás y a la larga ganarás más que en otras cosas, pues lo más productivo de la vida es lo más inútil. A la corta una notaría da dinero, y la literatura no da más que calentamientos de cabeza; pero a la larga la notaría sigue siendo notaría, y la literatura puede ser personalidad, esto es, existencia independiente y hasta ganancias metálicas, si se quiere explotar el filón. Si yo pudiera vivir en Granada, lo haría; me contentaría con un par de duros diarios y un poco menos; y quien sabe si aún podré conseguirlo, cambiando de rumbo. Por ahora, si sigo amarrado a este destino, es porque si lo dejo, no queriendo vivir a costa de nadie, no sé cómo iba a arreglarme para comer. (NML, 93-4)

In the letter of January 20 to Rafael Gago he addresses the issue of literary critics and older, established authors who do nothing to further the careers of aspiring young writers. «Se respeta a los viejos, que ya dieron lo que tenían que dar y que van de capa caída; pero, al que puede dar algo, se le apabulla, si se puede» (LSLP, 121).

Just a few weeks later Ganivet wrote to López encouraging him in his poetic endeavors and advising him to disregard negative criticism: «Claro está que en los comienzos te pondrán dificultades, porque ahí se han empeñado en que no haya poetas; pero esto no debe asustarte, y si por acaso algún crítico te da un palo, miel sobre hojuelas» (NML, 90). Just two months later, in April, again to López, Ganivet expounds on the potentially positive, informative role that literary criticism can have:

> La crítica puede ser buena y útil cuando *da a conocer* las cosas, cuando ejerce de comadrona, y ensancha el horizonte intelectual de la Sociedad; sin esa crítica el Trabajo del que crea se quedaría en el limbo. Lo que es despreciable y perjudicial es la crítica de oficio, negativa y mal intencionada por lo general, de los Clarines y demás patulea. (NML, 96)

incident and Pío Cid emerges as a remarkably understanding and self-assured character.

Pío Cid's definition of artistic creation, which helps to explain the epithet «infatigable creador» of the novel's title and of Pío Cid's benevolent understanding of his disciple's unrequited love for Martina, also emerges from these exchanges with Gandaria. The internal and external, or personal and national origins of art, may be distinguished here. Pío Cid explains to the apprentice poet that the pain of a frustrated love is a certain source of creativity:

> Los espíritus delicados no sanan tan fácilmente, y una herida en el corazón, menos; en el amor propio, se les encona, y si cura les deja una huella indeleble. Y cuantas veces se pone el dedo en la herida, creación tenemos segura. Así es el hombre, todos los hombres, y usted como los demás. (II, 258).

Anyone capable of loving, Pío Cid continues, is a poet, a creator, whose artistic vision is as large or small as the object of his love. A family is the typical creation of most human love. If, however, an individual's love is frustrated, the result can be another broader, more spiritual creation: «en el origen del arte humano, en la formación del alma creadora del hombre, hay eternamente una revulsión del amor natural, sin la que este amor no se remontaría a la contemplación pura de los seres» (II, 260).

Pío Cid explains that the artist's finest creations arise from a refinement of human passions mixed with spirituality: «lo humano no es lo sensual ni lo corpóreo, sino la fusión de esto y de lo espiritual, la vena de sentimiento puro, sin escoria, del que sacamos nuestras mayores creaciones» (II, 239). These creations are not limited to literature, music, or the plastic arts: «un poeta es un creador que se sirve de todos los medios humanos de expresión, entre los que la acción ocupa quizá más alto lugar que las formas artísticas más conocidas: las palabras, los sonidos, los colores» (II, 256). Pío Cid discovers in Purilla's selfless dedication to the sick an example of a superior poetic creation.

Pío Cid presents the external source of art as being the national artistic tradition. He enlists Gandaria's creative energies by appealing to his patriotism. Spain's intellectual prestige is at a low ebb, he tells him, and Spain's sons must take it upon themselves to revitalize it. Employing a wonderful reference to the classical world, Pío Cid tells Gandaria: «Siga el ejemplo de los pequeños mirmidones que para ser grandes bailaban sobre la tumba de Aquiles. Baile usted encima de todas nuestras glorias nacionales» (II, 256). Thus Pío Cid, himself described in *La conquista* as «el más original caballero andante que se haya visto en el mundo,» sees artistic strength arising from youth's reinterpretation of Spain's masterpieces —a reinterpretation Ganivet and other members of the Generation of '98 were to attempt with considerable success.

Not only is Gandaria transformed by his relations with Pío Cid, thus discovering his true vocation, but his younger sister Consuelo is equally affected. In this young woman Pío Cid senses a religious spirit which he nourishes until her vocation is so clearly defined that she enters a convent. In their conversations also recorded in the third *trabajo,* Pío Cid's own spiritual, almost Christ-like nature (although unsupported by faith) is revealed. «El único sentimiento que yo soy capaz de sentir», he tells Consuelo, «es el amor, y lo siento por cuantas personas conozco» (II, 206). His understanding of this love, which social conventions prevent him from fully expressing, is simple: never consider using one's fellow creatures for one's own gain.

Pío Cid's spiritual character is underscored by the priestly role he assumes with Consuelo, imposing on her a penance of praying the litany and serving in their conversations together as her confessor. In their last meeting Pío Cid confides to Consuelo that were it not for his lack of faith he would become a monk to preserve his love of the soul from the encroachments of banal social obligations and commitments. Indeed, since childhood he had been drawn to convents to hear the nuns at prayer. For him their songs were not only hymns of faith but also hymns of contempt for a society that values purposeless agitation. And he remarks that but for his pacific nature and habits of contemplation he might well have become a revolutionary. The similarity of this often cited passage with Ganivet's letter of October 15, 1895, to his sisters who were considering a life in the convent after the death of their mother is striking and further reveals the deeply contemplative and spiritual nature of the author (CFAG, 256-7).

A farewell poem that Pío Cid writes in Consuelo's autograph book provides additional insight into his view of existence and art. The poem employs the image of a dead tree and a lively vine. The poet is represented by the tree, illusion is symbolized by the vine. The end of the poem finds the vine, which has embraced the tree, similarly overcome by death. Consuelo appreciates the truth in this nihilistic vision, although she would have found a happy ending more «natural.» But she realizes the autobiographical aspect of the poem and sees that someone who thinks this way «debe tener en su alma un vacío inmenso que asusta» (II, 220). She has compassion for this man who appears to be lacking joy, faith, hope, illusion, ambition —like the dead tree in his poem. Yet she is struck by his desire to strengthen the beliefs of others. Pío Cid's response suggests that he does possess exalted ideals, but not the narrow, conventional ones. He labors to help all those who undertake spiritual tasks but he does not attempt to impose «una idea personal y mezquina» (II, 222) upon them:

> ¿Cómo se concibe que un hombre irreligioso trabaje en pro de la religión unas veces, y otras en contra de ella, y que ese hombre no se mueva sin rumbo fijo, sino que sea tan firme e inconmovible como el árbol muerto, que muerto sigue clavado en tierra, mientras algunas de sus raíces están quizá echando retoños? Esto ocurre porque la muerte es fecunda y crea la vida, aunque sea sólo para entretenerse con ella; y un hombre que llevase la muerte absoluta dentro de su espíritu, y que se viera obligado a trabajar, sería un creador portentoso, porque no teniendo ya ideas de vida, que siempre son pequeñas y miserables, crearía con ideas de muerte, que son más amplias y nobles. (II, 221)

Death, then, is a creative force for Pío Cid and he teaches both Adolfo and Consuelo Gandaria—their surname must be symbolic of a wasteland, *gándara,* which can still, like the dead tree, produce a «retoño»—that death of love, of illusion or of faith can lead to profound and noble creations, works of art.

Pío Cid's foray into public life in the longest *trabajo,* the fourth, «Pío Cid emprende la reforma política de España,» seems surprising for a man who believes contemplation to be the highest human activity and who despises the parliamentary system of Spain. Yet, Ganivet portrays his protagonist's entry into politics as a means of achieving freedom from social conventions —as a Member of Parliament, he and the woman who shares his life will be respected, despite the irregular, extra-legal and extra-religious nature of their bond.

Pío Cid's election trip to the province of Granada presents a lively portrait of rural Andalusia: picturesque characters, customs and language, as well as instances of chronic poverty and injustice and the *caciquismo* that dominated provincial Restoration Spain. Pío Cid, the last descendant of a prominent local family, demonstrates an unfailing concern for the common people of his district and generosity toward them, and improves the lot of several individuals. In his only political speech, he summons his peasant audience to a kind of passive resistance against the *cacique* and suggests emigration if they cannot find work and respect in their village. Rather than trying to remedy the poisoned political situation of this town, Pío Cid advises his audience to know their place and not attempt to change it. The conservatism of his message is clear (and similar to what he had told Purilla) as he warns his listeners that their desire to rise in the social hierarchy only facilitates their domination.

But more importantly, Pío Cid means to bestow honor upon the secure existence of those who live close to the land, and on the special position they hold in the life of the nation. With the exception of a few rare individuals, Pío Cid tells his audience, human beings are lost when they cut their ties to the land; they become engulfed by loneliness and live in cities «como pájaros presos en la jaula,» frustrated and hungering for freedom. Those who remain on the land

> sois los más felices, los más humanos y los más grandes. No hay edad más dichosa que aquella en que el niño está mamando, en que para él no existe más gloria que estar colgado del pecho de su madre; y no hay condición más feliz que la del hombre que vive apegado a la tierra, madre de todos, recibiendo de ella la vida en pago de sus esfuerzos... El campesino... mientras vive no pierde el calor de su madre. (II, 366-7)

When confronted by life's tribulations they can draw strength and an enlarged perspective from their beautiful natural surroundings, diminishing the pain of evil and injustice. Thus, Ganivet urges inaction and the contemplation of nature.

In the closing line of this speech, Pío Cid, now a newly elected Member of Parliament, tells his constituents that happiness, which they expect to descend from heaven to earth, might well rise from the earth to the heavens and that they should add to the *Padrenuestro* a new prayer, the «Madre nuestra,» to the earth, «para rogar a la tierra que recompense con los frutos de su seno inagotable el esfuerzo de los que en ella trabajan» (II, 368).[10] These words, like the rest of the speech, so full of nostalgia for an all but lost existence and of affirmation of personal and spiritual values, hardly suggest a political discourse (one of the listeners appropriately calls it a «sermón»).[11] And, true to the spirit of the speech, Pío Cid swiftly changes course. Two days later he renounces his election and cedes his seat in Parliament to his opponent.

The narrator says the decision was made on the way back to Granada after the election, shortly after Pío Cid gave his speech and probably while he climbed the imposing Mount Veleta, one of the highest peaks of the Sierra Nevada.[12] There at dawn, another intimate transformation took place similar to the one which occurred when he met Martina, although this one somewhat eclipses the earlier one, as Pío Cid here seems to move away from the love of a mortal woman when he has a presentiment of «la visión blanca,» «el ideal de pureza y de amor y de justicia que él no hallaba en el mundo» (II, 376).[13].

This episode is never further elaborated in the remaining completed chapters, despite the promised future importance of the white vision in Pío Cid's life. But its appearance does indicate a change in the character's perceptions and helps to explain Pío Cid's sudden withdrawal from public life.

An illumination of this withdrawal can be found in Ganivet's letter of November 17, 1893, to Navarro. Here Ganivet comments on the type of solitary man who does not want to fight, but when he does is victorious and then chooses to withdraw. The common folk, Ganivet went on, think everyone who lays down his arms has been defeated; they do not recognize in anyone an «espíritu excepcional» whose dissatisfaction is not the result of ambition for higher posts, nor «por cansancio moral ni físico, ni por cobardía, ni por desaliento, ni por egoísmo, sino por repugnancia natural a un orden establecido» (II, 922). Pío Cid shares this repugnance with his creator.

Another facet of Pío Cid's removal from the political arena is that it is a precursor to situations repeated in later novels by members of

[10] Similarly to Ganivet in the *Idearium*, Pío Cid holds that: «de la tierra no salen sólo minerales ni brotan sólo plantas; salen ideas y brotan sentimientos...» (II, 368), an idea quite in keeping with his views on artistic creation expressed here and in *Libro de Granada*.

[11] A. A. Parker, «The novels...», 376-7, comments that the novel's tone is «didactic» and «evangelical» and «often recalls the Gospels.»

[12] See Antón del Sauce (Nicolás María López), «De pie con Ganivet,» in *Viajes románticos de Antón del Sauce* (Granada, 1932), for information about a probable model for Pío Cid's electoral journey in Andalusia.

[13] JH, 169-74, offers an original interpretation of this episode and concludes that in the passage on Mount Veleta: «La Niña Blanca (o Hija de Oriente) que el alma persigue es el símbolo de la Belleza ideal (o del mundo de las Ideas), trascendente.»

the Generation of 1898. Among these, Baroja's César Moncada in *César o nada* (1910) most closely resembles Pío Cid in that he, too, conceives of politics as a personal quest, also based on a type of personal charisma rather than a commitment to social change through long-term group effort and an understanding of economic, social, and political reality. After a setback, César also withdraws from public life and devotes himself to his private art collection.[14] Both Pío Cid and César attain positions of political power, yet both flee politics to dedicate themselves to more subjective satisfactions.[15] Although by withdrawing from public life they tacitly serve to perpetuate unjust conditions, by engaging in politics at all they have called attention to the corruption of their nation's politicians and to their pernicious effects on the lives of Spaniards. But whatever the political import of the novel, it is clear that Ganivet is concerned throughout this as well as his other works primarily with man's internal, spiritual state and with the creations that arise from it. Ganivet, like other members of the Generation of '98, was an artist-intellectual, not a politician and, though they were all moved to varying degrees by the injustices and lack of direction of their once glorious nation, they were not destined to change them.

In the fifth *trabajo,* «Pío Cid acude a levantar a una mujer caída,» the protagonist, before returning to Madrid, spends an afternoon and evening in Granada with his literary and artistic friends, who comprise a novelistic version of the *Cofradía del Avellano.*[16] He reads his prescription for curing intellectual sloth and chides his friends for not bringing their literary projects to fruition (a probable reference to the slow progress of Ganivet's colleagues on the *Libro de Granada*). At the insistence of a friend he labels his prescription *Ecce homo,* recalling Nietzsche's book of the same title, and signaling «he aquí el hombre apto para crear obras útiles,» what he offers is a «retrato de un hombre de voluntad.»[17]

[14] The first edition of this novel has this ending, but not the Biblioteca Nueva edition of 1946-1951 which omits the final chapter.

[15] Carlos Blanco Aguinaga's challenging *Juventud del 98* (Madrid, 1970), was among the first to criticize members of the Generation of 1898 (although not specifically Ganivet) for their failure to provide leadership in the public sector and for their retreat into solipsism.

[16] See Agudiez, *Las novelas...,* 144-5, for a fuller description of the novelistic portrayal of the *Cofradía.*

[17] Gonzalo Sobejano, *Nietzsche en España,* 271, states: «Es este segundo Pío Cid el que fue tomado por algunos contemporáneos y por ciertos críticos posteriores como una especie de encarnación española del superhombre, sin duda por su fuerte independencia individualista, su nueva moral autárquica, su voluntarismo prometeico y la curativa dureza con que trata a los hombres y se trata a sí mismo. En propiedad poco puede tener de 'superhombre' un personaje tan contradictorio y, en lo íntimo, tan impregnado de compasión y saturado de nihilismo. Pero lo que sí encarna Pío Cid, acaso no por sugestión nietzscheana, sino de un modo espontáneo, es el 'espíritu libre,' el 'Freigeist,' definido por Nietzsche... como aquel hombre que piensa de manera diferente a como se esperaría de él por su origen, ambiente, clase y profesión o por los criterios dominantes en su tiempo...», JH, 281-3, offers a comprehensive interpretation of the Arimi acrostic which opens the speech. The initial line, «Artis initium dolor,»

The wisdom Pío Cid offers in this speech is the wisdom he has lived by: to not allow society and its conventions to bother one, to disdain maternal concerns and wordly power, to practice personal charity rather than attempting large-scale social reforms, to combine audacity and discretion in one's actions with depth and breadth in one's view of the world, and above all, to cultivate the soul, both one's own and that of others. Humanity, he assures his listeners, can be changed by ideas or «invenciones intelectuales» which although at first they may be in conflict with reality, will eventually give fruit and create a new conception of life (II, 440).

Pío Cid's «retrato» also includes a prescription for living with others, one that not only he but Angel the narrator in emulation of him followed. Pío Cid urges his friends to establish a «natural» family of «voluntad y de ideas» in place of the «familia de sangre y de intereses» that so often serves to justify outrageously selfish behavior. This natural family must be open to anyone who wants to reside within it, regardless of what he or she may offer in return, since by such generous actions one becomes «más hombre.» Do not delay in forming this family, joining your life with a woman of the people, he says; do it at once in a union of true spiritual energy that will lift you to the heights of contemplation. And do not fear the want of resources; you will have enough. Finally, strengthening the elegiac tone that particularly marks the speech, Pío Cid tells his friends that they should not concern themselves with their future importance but only with the example of their lives and the influence of their personalities, «que es el único testamento que debe dejar un hombre honrado» (II, 439).

The speech breaks off with a few words on the nobility of redeeming a fallen woman through love and a hint that more can be done for her than redemption. But there, with yet another allusion to Jesus, Pío Cid ends his talk, leaving his audience in doubt. Although Pío Cid provides no further information on this theme in the speech, Ganivet has him imitate Jesus's gesture toward Mary Magdalena when Pío Cid invites Mercedes, the fallen daughter of Juanico el Ciego whom he meets on the train back to Madrid, to come and live with his family. Unlike the gospel story, however, this gesture leads to domestic conflict and illuminates the relation between Pío Cid and Martina. By following his charitable precepts and opening his home to Mercedes, Pío Cid causes Martina to resent the presence of another woman (and a very beautiful one) in her household. Beset by this resentment, Martina manages to foster an illicit liaison between Mercedes and Gandaria, and this results in the fallen woman's exit from the house and the frustration of Pío Cid's attempt to redeem her and to help her escape from her seemingly inevitable destiny.

reaffirms the statements to Gandaria about creativity in the third *trabajo*. In his «Declaración» in «Epistolario,» *Revista de Occidente* 11 (1965), 321, written two days before his suicide, Ganivet wrote: «Mis ideas prácticas sobre la vida están expuestas en mi novela *Los Trabajos de Pío Cid,* en particular en el 'Ecce Homo.' Tal como lo he pensado lo he practicado siempre...»

Nonetheless, Mercedes, too, is transformed internally by her contact with Pío Cid and her transformation is one of Pío Cid's *trabajos*, another example of the kind of «transformación íntima» that represents accomplishment for Ganivet-Pío Cid. As he retorts to Martina's complaint that Mercedes is a «huésped perpetuo» who does nothing: «... esa criatura, que está aquí sin ocuparse de nada al parecer, está haciendo algo que vale muchísimo. Acuérdate de cómo era cuando llegó y cómo es hoy... eso es lo que está haciendo: cambiarse. No todos los trabajos tienen nombre, y aunque Mercedes no hiciera absolutamente nada más que estar aquí, haría algo que, aunque no se viera, no por eso valdría menos» (II, 533).[18]

The Mercedes episode makes evident how dissimilar Pío Cid and Martina are. Martina in a number of ways, especially in her literal-mindedness and fondness for «refranes,» is an earthy foil, a Sancho Panza figure to Pío Cid's spiritual Don Quixote-like character. Unlike Pío Cid, Martina is possessive and jealous, uninterested in intellectual or artistic pursuits, and believes that women should simply marry and have pretty babies: «lo demás son tonterías» (II, 271).[19] In the sixth *trabajo,* «Pío Cid asiste a una enferma de frivolidad,» Pío Cid tells the «sufferer,» the Duchess Soledad de Almadura, that Martina is «humana,» «la vulgaridad personificada,» a woman who is «la realidad pura.» He also suggests —as he did in the fifth *trabajo*— that such a woman is necessary and good for a man despite the troubles she brings him. A woman, he tells the Duchess, should be like the earth, and a man like a tree, each dependent on the other. As a treeless terrain becomes barren and sterile, so, too, the roots of a tree, when deprived of soil, will wither and die. A woman anchors a man to reality and prevents him from losing himself in «estériles idealismos.» Conversely, a man protects a woman with «la sombra de sus ideas» so that she does not deteriorate, as she would if left alone at the mercy of the elements (II, 542-3).

Much of this last *trabajo* is devoted to Pío Cid's role as confessor to the Duchess and as tutor to her son Jaime. Several familiar themes are played again: Spain must not be a servile imitator of other nations whose abuse of material strength bespeaks an obvious inferiority to Spain; the formation of a child's spirit is a work of art that must be achieved individually, and this work is of greater value than governing; teaching must also strive to awaken in the child an appreciation of the interrelatedness of the human community. More importantly, however, is

[18] I am indebted to Professor Rizel Sigele for pointing out the interesting similarities between the characters of Mercedes and that of Fortunata in Galdós' *Fortunata y Jacinta* which Ganivet read and praised.

[19] Martina's view of books further characterizes her as an instinctual not an intellectual being, «todos esos librotes, hoy unos y mañana otros, todos servirán para envolver» (II, 531). A fine study of the portrait of the Spanish ideal of womanhood in the second half of the nineteenth century (one which would be consonant with Martina's statements) is by Bridget Aldaraca, «El ángel del hogar: The Cult of Domesticity in Nineteenth-Century Spain,» in G. Mora and K. Van Hooft, eds., *Theory and Practice of Feminist Literary Criticism* (Ypsilanti, Michigan, Bilingual Press, 1982), 62-87.

the final elaboration in the sixth *trabajo* of the themes of love and creativity which close the completed portion of the novel and prefigure Ganivet's play, *El escultor de su alma.*

Through the relationship of Pío Cid and the Duchess, Ganivet demonstrates both the superiority of spiritual over carnal love and the birth of creativity from the former when the latter is redirected. One of Pío Cid's ways of communicating with the Duchess is through art —poetry and portraiture. Pío Cid presents the Duchess with a portrait he has made of her— one that complements the *Ecce homo,* the «retrato de un hombre de voluntad» that he shared with his friends in the fifth *trabajo.* The feminine portrait consists of two parts: a sonnet, which corresponds to the preliminary sketch, and a small, perfectly executed pencil drawing of the Duchess. The use of two media reflects Pío Cid's impressive breadth as an artist; the use of pencil, in intentional contrast to a pretentious and superficial oil painting of the same subject by an «artista de gran fama,» denotes the *sencillez* of his art. This portrait, like the *Ecce homo,* is offered as a guide to living for its recipient. Here, Pío Cid suggests a remedy for this narcissistic and unhappy aristocrat, uninterested in her son and trapped in a marriage of convenience —maternal love. Pío Cid's drawing is based on «reality» in that he has faithfully duplicated a photograph the Duchess had loaned him. However, to this reality the artist, «el creador,» has added his vision —the Duchess nursing a contented infant. «No hay para la mujer refugio más seguro que el amor maternal,» Pío Cid insists. «¡Cuántas mujeres, quizá usted misma, sufren el hastío de la vida porque buscan la felicidad en frívolos pasatiempos, cuando la hallarían en el amor de madre!» (II, 551-2).

Initially, the Duchess cannot accept the message of Pío Cid's didactic art; she is unable to love the child of a man for whom she feels contempt and who has humiliated her with implicit but false accusations of infidelity and equally untrue forgiveness. In further conversations with the Duchess, an understanding Pío Cid defends «los derechos del corazón» that justify a woman to break free from false and demeaning conjugal obligations. And he tells the Duchess that her husband's unjust accusations give cause for action since the appearance of a misdeed is worse than the misdeed itself. At least something positive could come from the misdeed, because it is real; only fictions can come from appearances. Foreshadowing Freud's understanding of the power of human drives, Pío Cid explains that when one cannot forgive another or resign oneself to a situation, it is better to allow one's passion expression in a censurable act than to poison oneself in mute, inner protest. After all, Pío Cid says, a «falta» is a human thing that may help one gain insight and strength to achieve higher aims.

In another original reworking of the traditional Spanish theme of honor, Pío Cid also speaks with equanimity of the importance of this virtue for society and of the balance that must be maintained between society's need for honor and the individual's need for love. Here the unconventionality of Ganivet-Pío Cid's conception of the relations between the sexes is given yet another application. Infidelity is neither championed nor excoriated, but is seen in terms of the individual's unavoidable weaknesses and necessities, society's reasonable demands, and the desirability of an equilibrium between them.

Although Pío Cid acknowledges the tremendous importance of love in a woman's life, he also asserts that there is something greater than love: «... pero para llegar a ello no hay más camino que el amor. El mejor amor es el espiritual, y si éste no basta, el amor corpóreo... yo no siento ya más amor que el espiritual, y aun éste con trabajo» (II, 544-5).

Thus, it is clear that Pío Cid is not responsible for the Duchess' subsequent infidelity, despite the fact that in the last pages of the text the Duchess briefly eases her own conscience by blaming his liberal counsel for her «falta.» A closer examination of his conversations with the Duchess reveals that Pío Cid is actually encouraging her creative powers by advising her to confront the truth of her unhappy situation. Pain, he tells her, and the reader recalls what he had earlier told Gandaria, can only be overcome by transforming it into something else:

> Más vale afrontar la verdad entera, porque, aunque la verdad sea dolorosa, el dolor es fecundo y crea alegrías que las agradables ficciones no crearán jamás. Si usted sufre, declárese a sí misma, sin engañarse, cuál es su sufrimiento; recójase y medite luego sobre él y verá salir de él un deseo que la llevará, como de la mano, a un placer nuevo, desconocido y tan hondo como el sufrimiento que lo ha engendrado. (II, 552)

When Pío Cid leaves the Duchess' company for the last time, she, like so many other characters in the novel —Consuelo, Purilla, Gandaria —has been transformed internally through her contact with him. The reader senses that she is about to create something through her self-discovery and the contemplation and mastery of her pain, as have the other characters. As a result of Pío Cid's parting words, a «canción amorosa,» the Duchess' dormant maternal love is awakened and she is in a state of «sereno éxtasis» after which she finds herself in a «mundo nuevo, ideal y soñado... se preguntaba a sí misma quién era aquella mujer que dentro de ella estaba y que le parecía una criatura nueva en el mundo» (II, 562-3).[20]

In the last pages of the novel, immediately after the Duchess has committed adultery for the first time, she receives a final message from Pío Cid, a poetic dialogue between «El Enamorado» and «La Sombra» which is named «Soledad,» after her. The poem is described as «una alegoría, cuyo sentido íntimo escapaba a la penetración de la duquesa» (II, 573). Nonetheless, she receives it as a «gota de bálsamo... aunque el efecto que le produjo fue de arrepentimiento por el mal paso que acababa

[20] The Duchess' state corresponds strikingly to Ganivet's own in October of 1896, which he described to López:

> Y salgo a catástrofe moral por semana, y me va bien; el corazón se me va convirtiendo en un guijarro, pero siento como si me naciera un nuevo corazón más sutil, gaseoso, difundido por todo mi cuerpo, que me trae una sensibilidad nueva, la del instinto, y un amor más grande, que se parece al que deben gozar las almas de los que murieron... (NML, 72)

de dar, y de nueva y más honda desilusión por el amor de los hombres...» (II, 573). Again, Pío Cid has chosen poetry as his medium of communication with the Duchess; again, he appears to be offering her both her portrait and a guide for her spirit; again, art and love are the themes of Pío Cid's creation; and again, Ganivet has chosen to end a novel about Pío Cid with an allegory which captures the essence of the whole book.

La Sombra is what remains of carnal love:

> Ya no hay fuego ni amor;
> sólo queda una sombra en un desierto:
> el desierto es el frío de la vida
> y la sombra es el humo de las almas.
> ....
> me quedas tú en el mundo, Sombra amada.
> Muere el amor, mas queda su perfume. (II, 574)

La Sombra is durable and lasting, unlike carnal love:

> todo murió; más tú no me abandones
> ... Mi amor es siempre tuyo.
> Como no tienes cuerpo, eres eterna. (II, 575)

La Sombra will accompany *El Enamorado* wherever he goes; she is a spiritual creation and she is also an artistic creation:

> Voy lejos, no sé adónde;
> mas no voy sólo, tú vas junto a mí.
> Vas flotando, flotando
> como una sombra que eres,
> una estatuta esculpida en noble espíritu,
> pura idea de amor
> con larga cabellera luminosa. (II, 575)

The statue, the work of art, is a purification, a spiritualization of love. This statue also seems to represent carnal love between the Duchess and Pío Cid, which has been turned into a superior spiritual, artistic creation. We recall the kiss the Duchess gave Pío Cid just before he sang his «canción amorosa» to her and how at the time Pío Cid had imagined that the Duchess, who has fainted after the kiss, «no estaba desmayada, sino muerta y convertida en estatuta yacente» (II, 560). Further, since the Duchess has been described as «más bien rubia,» her face set off by a «marco que formaban los oscuros bucles cayendo flotantes en estudiado desorden» (II, 524), the possibility that the statue refers to her seems a convincing one, especially when it is recalled that the poem is entitled «Soledad» and the Duchess appears as a statue, a work of art which is purely spiritual. This interpretation gains greater force when we note that in his next creative work, *El escultor de su alma,* a similar female sculpture also represents a love that has been redirected into art. Pío Cid's own experience is reflected in this movement away from carnal toward spiritual love and he has led those with whom he has come into contact toward ever more spiritual manifestations of love. Martina's carnal love for Pío Cid becomes transformed into maternal love for her twins. Consuelo's religious vocation is an acceptance of a spiritual love. Purilla's selfless dedication to others is yet another example of the purification of love, which creates art.

Los trabajos is Ganivet's most interesting and important work, despite the greater fame of the *Idearium,* and it possesses a freshness that the better known work lacks. The innovations introduced in the novel —its intellectually self-aware protagonist, its lack of external description and dramatic conflict, and the enormous importance of dialogue— are, as Shaw has convincingly demonstrated, salient characteristics of the novel of the Generation of 1898 and were to reappear significantly in the later novels of Unamuno and Baroja.[21] What separates *Los trabajos* from these later novels, however, is its rebelious criticism of the constrictive morality of the day, its proclamation of the highly unconventional «natural family,» and its exploration of artistic creativity. A dramatic illustration of how different Ganivet's boldly original view of Spanish society was from the conventions of his time is the fact that although *Los trabajos* was praised by Ganivet's friends and other more progressive readers, it was considered «immoral and scandalous» in Granada when it was first published: Ganivet's uncle, charged with distributing copies to his nephew's friends, destroyed the remaining ones when he learned of its reputation.[22]

Los trabajos also has a special biographical interest because of its treatment of suicide. Ganivet's subsequent suicide thus appears prefigured in this context. In *trabajos* IV and V, for example, Pío Cid makes several allusions to his own death: he is certain he will not return alive to Granada and, as he unexpectedly ends his *Ecce homo* speech, he tells his friends that upon his death, which will be soon, the speech's conclusion will be revealed in a tragedy that he as already written, a tragedy which is the «tragedia invariable de la vida» (II, 444).[23] This public, albeit veiled, acknowledgment of suicide, written less than a year before Ganivet took his life, supports Herrero's contention that Ganivet's decision to kill himself had been made well before the event.[24] Although it is beyond the scope of this study to submit the author's life and work to exhaustive psychoanalytic scrutiny, there are nonetheless many elements in *Los trabajos* which would provide fruitful terrain for a psychoanalytic interpretation of Ganivet's life.

The persistent association of Pío Cid and Jesus Christ strongly suggests a pathologically grandiose self image which would be in keeping with Utrillo's impressions of Ganivet when the two met in Barcelona in the late summer of 1897. Such an omnipotent self-image would be impossible to maintain and the inability, failure, or perceived refusal of the outside world to support such a self-image has long been associated

21 *The Generation,* 31-3; 53.

22 Gómez Moreno, «Recuerdos de un condiscípulo,» 330. See also NML, 101, and López, «Ganivet y sus obras,» 18.

23 In Ganivet's outline of the unfinished *trabajos* published in GM:ET, 47, the «muerte de Pío Cid» occurs in the twelfth *trabajo.*

24 JH, 267-70.

with suicide attempts in neurotically depressed individuals.[25] The prayer to «Nuestra Madre» in *trabajo* IV, in addition to its significance as part of a speech which reflects a deeply conservative view of politics, and as an indication of profound nostalgia for Granada, also lends itself to a psychoanalytic interpretation as the expression of the author's longing for union with an omnipotent mother. Other indications of this would be found in the exaltation of maternal love and the portrait of the Duchess in *trabajo* VI. This type of longing has also been clinically linked with suicide attempts which are viewed as efforts to achieve this union.[26]

This interpretation acquires greater force when major events of Ganivet's early years are recalled —the death of his father, his accident, the long period of recuperation in the mill in Granada with his mother, his grandfather's paralysis and the many summer excursions with his mother to take medicinal baths. The death of his father, his winning of the oedipal struggle, may have elicited powerful feelings of guilt and ambivalence. The paralysis that immobilized his maternal grandfather (a surrogate father) could also have reactivated the conflicts raised by the earlier loss. Psychiatrists have also found a pattern, «the death trend,» in persons who have lost a parent or sibling before the end of adolescence and who subsequently commit suicide.[27] The incidence of twentieth-century artists whose fathers died when they were children and who were later victims of suicide is striking: Ernest Hemingway, Valdimir Mayakovsky, Cesare Pavese and Sylvia Plath.

«*Hombres del norte*»

Upon his return to Helsinki in September of 1897 after a summer in Spain, Ganivet informed Francisco Seco de Lucena, an editor of *El Defensor,* that he intended to write a series of essays on Norwegian literature under the title *Hombres del norte,* which he hoped later to publish in a book for the general public (LSLP, 98). A year later, while in Riga, he added a promise to include essays on Russian authors as well. He never wrote the Russian essays despite repeated expressions of his intention to do so. But he assured Seco de Lucena in the letter of January 26, 1898, that accompanied his first article (one he had hoped to finish in November but had been delayed by Ganivet's preoccupation with *Los trabajos),* that whatever he wrote would not be mere novelty pieces but substantive articles: «... yo no quiero escribir siluetillas en que se da

25 See, for example, the classic psychoanalytic text, OTTO FENICHEL, *The Psychoanalytic Theory of Neurosis* (New York: Norton, 1945), 401-5. A. ALVAREZ, *The Savage God: A Study of Suicide* (New York, 1971), offers a review of the theories of suicide, society's evaluation of the act in different eras and studies of the notion in a number of authors who either contemplated or attempted self-destruction.

26 FENICHEL, *The Psychoanalytic...*, 401-5.

27 ALVAREZ, *The Savage God,* 108-11.

más importancia al detalle simplemente curioso que a lo fundamental» (LSLP, 100, 110).

The first article —on Jonas Lie (1833-1908)— appeared on February 4, 1898. It was followed over the next six months by five more on Bjornsterne Bjornson (1832-1910), Henrik Ibsen (1828-1906), Arne Garborg (1851-1924), Knut Hamsun (1859-1952) and Wilhelm Krag (1871-1933).[28] In October he informed Seco that he had started articles on Jens Peter Jacobson (1847-85), the Danish novelist and poet, and George Brandes (1842-1927), the Danish critic and literary historian, and that in December he hoped to write on the Swedish poets and novelists Viktor Rydberg (1828-95) and Verner Heidenstam (1859-1940). None of these four materialized, or they were lost in transit, for they never arrived in Granada and were not found after Ganivet's death among his papers.

Hombres del norte is of particular interest as Ganivet's last public statements on European literature. Again, as in *Cartas finlandesas,* Ganivet wants to share with his countrymen what he has learned about the culture and, particularly, the literature of the northern countries. But he is also careful to disclaim any attempt to introduce «new» influences into Spanish art; he wants only to educate and hopes the work will have a wider audience than the circle of friends in Granada for whom he originally wrote *Cartas finlandesas* (LSLP, 98).

Ganivet's interest in the authors he examines here lies primarily in the intellectual content rather than formal qualities of their work. He does, however, exhibit some sensitivity to the balance between them. Not surprisingly, the author of the *Idearium* particularly praises authors like Jonas Lie, the «Norwegian Pereda,» who fully capture Norwegian life and its true national character, as well as the Nordic enthusiasm for fantasy and allegory that he considers an expression of the «espíritu poético territorial» of these frigid climes (II, 1024-5). His evaluations of these authors are respectful and well measured; they largely coincide with the criticism of them found in recent literary histories. He judges Bjornson a «romántico,» a «poeta natural,» who expresses himself with spontaneity rather than searching for form, and whom he credits with «el descubrimiento del verdadero carácter nacional» of Norway (II, 1034-5). He praises Hamsun for his «ideas frescas» and the breath and independence of his cultural background while criticizing his leadership in the decadent movement. Ganivet had long found decadentism to be misguided as a criticism of the then prevalent positivism. As he did in the *Idearium,* Ganivet here advocates strength and positive «fe en algo» rather than the weariness, doubt and sadness offered by decadentism.[29]

Ganivet terms Arne Garborg a «symptomatic writer» whose works have a greater value as indications of society's intellectual and senti-

[28] Only the first three of these are included in the *Obras* (II, 1021-56); they were originally published in *El Defensor,* 4 February, 2 March and 22-23 June, 1898. The last three were also originally published in *El Defensor,* 27 August, 23 July, and 30 August, respectively, and in the first edition of *Hombres del norte*; subsequent editions omit them but they are available in GM:ET, 24-33.

[29] *Ibid.,* 26.

mental state than as works of art. But he strongly affirms Garborg's pioneering use of Norwegian in his works and credits him with making it a literary language and thus adding a more specifically Norwegian character to the national cultural renaissance initiated by his predecessors.[30]

In his analysis of Ibsen, the longest of the six, Ganivet lauds the dramatist's affinities with Nietzsche as «un defensor exaltado del individuo contra la sociedad...» (II, 1043). His comment here that «para reformar la sociedad hay que reformar al individuo,» and that this can be achieved only by allowing the individual to struggle, regardless of the harm that might cause those less fit for the struggle, is in keeping with his view of how society operates, and his own Nietzschean inclinations prompt Ganivet to single out Ibsen's John Gabriel Borkman as an especially admirable creation: a man who is not part of a crowd, «un cualquiera» (II, 1048).

Besides his praise for Ibsen's views on society, Ganivet also dwells upon several other themes of perennial interest to him. He compliments the Norwegians who, in contrast to the Spanish, give prominence to their authors. In his essay on Krag he draws the distinction between the relative merits of aesthetically striking poetry and intellectually substantive poetry. Concluding that substance is necessary for greatness whether one has aesthetic ingenuity or not, he finds that Krag, while an ingenious poet, is also on the way to becoming a great one because of the new depth his work was taking on.

Ganivet also considers the attributes of drama as a social experience and an art form (he was at this time writing his play, *El escultor de su alma).* In the North, he says, the theatre serves a didactic function while in the South people go to the theatre seeking entertainment. Hence Southerners see and learn only what they perceived visually. For this reason Spanish theatre is not intellectual, but scenic, and Spanish symbolism is not conceptual, like Ibsen's, but a «simbolismo de acción,» as in Calderón's *La vida es sueño* (II, 1052). Logic, he continues, is not a dramatic quality; to achieve theatrical success it is necessary to create «an effect» by presenting situations that are in harmony with the audience's state of mind. But, curiously, considering his admiration for Ibsen, Ganivet did not consider social issues suited to the theatre because they became dated too quickly. Ganivet wanted his own works to be admired by posterity. Better suited to drama, and of lasting significance, are psychological issues, matters of the soul. And it was these that he addressed in his only play, *El escultor de su alma.*

30 *Ibid.*, 27-8.

Chapter 6

RIGA

In early 1898, following Ganivet's charge that the Spanish consulate in Helsinki was unnecessary, the Spanish government dismantled it and established a new one in Riga, Latvia, to handle the commercial shipping between Spain and Russia. It has also been suggested that Ganivet wanted to leave Helsinki because of his unhappy love affair with Mascha Djakoffsky.[1] Ganivet was named consul of this post in June, but he did not take it up until mid-August, little more than three months before his suicide on November 29. Since he had sent his sisters, Amelia, and his son back to Spain in July, he lived alone in Riga, although he appears to have made a number of friends in the short time he was there.

His first impressions of his new home were not enthusiastic. As large as Antwerp but livelier and more expensive, Riga struck Ganivet as inferior to the «tranquilo rinconcillo» that was Helsinki (NML, 99-100). The one advantage to his new surroundings was that he would be obliged to learn Russian. He did his best to reestablish the atmosphere he needed for work. He rented a house in the Hagenberg district, the most picturesque and quiet part of the city, similar to Helsinki's Brunsparken. His new home, which he thought of as a «retiro filosófico,» was near a pine forest, it had an enclosed garden, and it provided the solitude Ganivet so cherished, although, because of its location, to reach his office he had to take a short ferry ride across the Dvina, which he described as «soberbio.»

Unfortunately, little is known about Ganivet's life during the time he spent in Riga, although his brief stay there proved almost as productive as his time in Helsinki.[2] He appears to have commenced a work entitled *El dómine peregrino Don Rústico de Santafé,* of which only the briefest fragment remains, and he had briefly outlined a continuation of *Los trabajos del infatigable creador, Pío Cid* (GM: ET, 46-7). Yet another new project was a *Libro de Granada* for children, intended to replace the insipid readers used in grammar schools. He envisioned his

[1] See Gallego Morell, *Angel Ganivet*..., 140.

[2] The fullest account is in JH, 264-70. Herrero indicates that a nephew of Ganivet's possesses additional documentation that could add important information to our knowledge of this period. See also Gallego Morell, *Angel Ganivet*..., 173-181.

part of this collective work to be a group of science fiction-fantasy stories full of strange inventions that would awaken a child's originality and creativity (NML, 109-14). His letters and published writings of those months indicate that Ganivet remained intellectually occupied with the cultural condition of Spain, the end of her colonial empire, and her future aspirations. In addition to a routine consular report, «España y Rusia (Nuevos horizontes comerciales)» he composed a second group of essays on the future of Spain for *El Defensor* as part of his dialogue with Unamuno, and he absorbed news of the success of the *Idearium* and its French translation and of the dismal state of affairs in post-war Spain. While the disastrous morale of his defeated homeland greatly disturbed Ganivet, the impending loss of Cuba, Puerto Rico and the Philippines —to which he refers as «propiedades inútiles»— was almost a relief to him; he cites it as an example of how useful an opportune amputation can be[3] and he continued to maintain that regeneration would come only from within.

On September 16, *El Defensor* published his article «Nuestro espíritu misterioso,»[4] in which Ganivet urged his demoralized countrymen to discover their own mysterious spirit which alone could give birth to the «idea» that will revive the afflicted nation. As in the *Idearium,* the tone here is one of consolation: Ganivet portrays Spain's lost colonial power as a cyclone that, despite the damage it caused, has left the core of Spain's being untouched and still capable of producing the necessary inspiration for the nation. The colonial adventures were thus costly distractions that have made Spain stray from her own natural path (GM: ET, 8). Urging his compatriots to learn from their defeat, Ganivet invites them to imagine a new and original ideal emerging from the present ruins. He does not describe this ideal but merely says its creation will come not at the hands of politicians, missionaries, or soldiers, but at those of men who are «grandes y geniales escultores del espíritu» (GM: ET, 10).

Ganivet expanded upon this theme —and reworked ideas set forth in his books, especially *La conquista*— in an article entitled «¡Naññã!»[5] published in the magazine *Vida Nueva.* To civilize nations, he insisted, one must disregard conventional ideas as well as alien practices and beliefs, and labor, with cruelty if necessary, to enable human nature to become refined and purified, «según sus eternas leyes por interior metamorfosis» (GM: ET 12).

In mid-October, *Los trabajos,* written earlier that year and at the end of 1897, went on sale in Spain. At the same time, Ganivet sought to show gratitude to his supporters, who were promoting his reputation at home; an article of thanks in *El Defensor,* «Una idea,» October 26, 1898, is the last article of his to appear in his lifetime.[6] The «idea» presented

[3] Letter of May 17, 1898 in *Revista de Occidente,* II, 1965, 311-13.
[4] Not in *Obras,* but in GM: ET, 7-9.
[5] Not in *Obras,* but in GM: ET, 11-13.
[6] Not in *Obras,* but in GM: ET, 9-11. «Mis inventos» appeared in the Madrid newspaper *Vida Nueva* on 1 January 1899, and was the first of what was to have been a series for that publication. The article has not, to the best of my knowledge,

in this article was to have his play, *El escultor de su alma,* given its premiere in Granada and to devote the profits to celebrating the tricentennial of the birth of the *granadino* Alonso Cano (1601-1667), one of Spain's greatest sculptors of religious images. He especially wanted the play to be produced in Granada because it was to him a profoundly Granadan creation by virtue of its author, the place of its conception, the characters, and the setting (GM:ET, 10).

«Una idea» provides perhaps the most definitive context from which to date Ganivet's play *El escultor.* There is some uncertainty about the exact date of composition of this work, and scholars, particularly Herrero, have devoted some attention to the issue. Herrero believes that Ganivet wrote the verse drama shortly before writing *Los trabajos* and that at one time he contemplated inserting it into Part II of the novel, as Chapter IX, «Pío Cid acomete la renovación del teatro español.» Subsequently, according to Herrero, when Ganivet decided to commit suicide without having finished *Los trabajos,* he made the play an independent work (JH, 135-6).

Yet, in «Una idea» Ganivet tells his friends in Granada that their gift, a beautiful edition of *Las cartas,* «me coge con una obra sobre el yunque.» He admits that the work has been long on his mind, but not executed until now: «la pensé hace años antes de salir de Granada, y aunque la he puesto ahora, me he mantenido fiel a mi primer pensamiento» (GM:ET, 10). If Ganivet is to be believed, he had just completed the actual writing of the work which he mailed to Seco de Lucena on November 11, 1898 —just eighteen days before he took his life (LSLP, 113).[7]

Both in «Una idea» and in letters to Seco de Lucena and López, Ganivet warns his followers of the difficulties presented by the work. Aspiring through this play to revive the *auto sacramental,* Ganivet concedes that the resistance to such a genre is inherent in the realistic spirit of the time. He also notes that the verse form he used is not to current taste, which he dismisses as «malísimo» (LSLP, 113).

But these obstacles did not daunt Ganivet, and he did not want them to daunt his friends. At worst, he said, the play would serve Granada by breaking the ice for the development of a local theatre tradition, a logical consequence of his previously expressed admiration for the creativity of the ancient Greek and Italian Renaissance city states and his activity as initiator of the *Libro de Granada.* For if

been published in book form. Navarro's comment to Ganivet in a letter of October, 1898, that *Vida nueva* was not right for Ganivet is intriguing. See «Epistolario,» *Revista de Occidente,* II, no. 33 (1965), 318.

[7] The title of the play also underwent several transformations, as noted by Gallego Morell:

«*Creación drama místico en tres autos: Auto de la Fe, Auto del Amor, Auto de la Muerte compuesto en verso castellano por Angel Ganivet.* Otro: *Creación. Drama en tres autos: Fe, Amor, Muerte, escrito en verso por Angel Ganivet.* Un tercer título: *El impío Pedro Martín.* Una penúltima tentativa: *El escultor de su alma Pedro Mártir. Drama místico en tres autos: de la Fe, del Amor y de la Muerte, compuesto en verso castellano por Angel Ganivet,* título este último el más próximo al que se nos transmite como portada de la primera edición...» (GM:ET, 44).

Spain is to have her own theatre, this is the route she must follow (LSLP, 113).

Although he saw himself as an innovator, Ganivet said he had taken care in the play not to offend the local spirit of fervently Catholic Granada (NML, 108). The play's subject might be «delicate» and the protagonist might express a few strong ideas, but Ganivet assured Seco that the ending resolved all moral questions (LSLP, 113). In sum, the work was orthodox and «parece escrita por un creyente» (NML, 108).

Notwithstanding these assurances, Ganivet had doubts about the play's merits. Just as he had confessed uncertainty years earlier over his ability to gauge the sense and shape of *La conquista,* he confided to Seco that he may not have succeeded in giving adequate form to his latest idea (LSLP, 113-4). But, he said, the play must not be judged by reading; it must be seen on the stage. And to prevent it being misjudged, Ganivet twice asked Seco not to allow his manuscript to circulate, except among his closest friends, before the work was produced (LSLP, 112, 113). This instruction also betrays Ganivet's desire to create a distinctive and perhaps even surprising theatrical event in his native city —a desire further evidenced by his comments on the type and quality of the four actors needed, and on the requirements for costumes and sets.[8]

«*El escultor de su alma*»

El escultor de su alma, subtitled «drama místico», is composed of three brief acts, called *autos,* entitled «Auto de la fe,» «Auto del amor,» and «Auto de la muerte.» Its descendance from the *auto sacramental* and its affinity with the works of Lope and particularly with Calderón's *La vida es sueño*[9] are evident in the use of classic Spanish verse forms such as the *décima,* the ten-line stanza used most notably by Calderon, the *redondilla,* and the *romance.* The play deals with the struggle of the sculptor, Pedro Mártir,[10] to create himself and become immortal as an artist. His is the struggle of the individual longing to affirm himself against the existence or supremacy of God.

«La fe,» the first *auto,* takes place in a dimly lit, statue-filled subterranean room in one of the Alhambra's towers. As the play begins, Pedro, «el hombre natural,»[11] meditates, rather like Hamlet and Segismundo, on the puzzling nature of human existence. Passing in review the everchanging spectrum of human emotion and experience —love,

[8] See *El escultor de su alma,* edited by FRANCISCO SECO DE LUCENA (Madrid, 1926), 43, for the indications Ganivet made for the play's production and which are inexplicably omitted from the *Obras.*

[9] In the *Idearium* Ganivet calls *La vida es sueño* «una de las obras mayores de nuestro teatro... un caso psicológico individual que tiene un valor simbólico universal, nos da el artista una explicación clara, lúcida y profética de nuestra historia» (I, 278).

[10] Ganivet was born on Pedro Mártir Street in Granada.

[11] *El escultor,* ed. Seco, 43.

pain, pleasure, liberty— he concludes that the only stable reality is death. But he cannot resolve the confusion of illusion and reality in his life or the kindred ambiguity of the relation between God and his creatures. Sensing that the statues he has formed are devoid of any trace of himself, and merely «cáscaras huecas sin peso,» he wonders if the relationship between man and God is the same —one in which the creation carries nothing of the creator.

> ¿Son las humanas criaturas
> risibles caricaturas
> de una excelsa realidad,
> de una sublime verdad,
> como estas pobres figuras? (II, 736)

Abandoning his previous aspiration to create immortal works of art, he now views creation as an internal process and desires only to create one last, perfect statue that will embody his soul. This act of self-creation is to be carried out through the recently begun sculpture of his infant daughter, Alma, still only a «pedazo de barro informe» before him. Pedro then falls asleep embracing the clay. Cecilia,[12] his mistress and the infant Alma's mother, enters carrying a lighted candle. But the light that she brings, symbolic of her faith, is unable to illuminate the dark cave. Looking at her sleeping lover she understands that Pedro's embrace of the clay represents a rejection of both her and her God. When he awakens he reaffirms his decision to pursue his destiny as an artist. And he leaves her, the child, and Granada the following day.

Ganivet thus sets up an antinomy between the ideal of creating works of art and the ideal of a religious faith that requires the individual to sacrifice his identity to a superior being. The freedom that the artist demands, and which Pedro seeks, begins by positing the self as supreme, rejecting bonds of human love attaching him to persons and country, and denying the Divine Being.

«Amor,» the second and longest of the three *autos,* takes place in a garden at sunset, in view of the Alhambra's towers. Fifteen years have passed. In the opening scenes, Alma, a beautiful young woman,[13] tells her fiancé, Aurelio (la vanidad del mundo),[14] of her yearning to see her father whom she has never known. At that moment Pedro appears disguised as a beggar. He has returned to Granada impelled by instructions in a dream to give his daughter a precious diamond that represents his soul. His return symbolizes his readiness to complete the statue of Alma that he had left behind.

But years of travelling and suffering have not made Pedro wiser. Obsessed by an ideal of love superior to human love he allows himself to play out with Alma the old conflict between him and her mother. Alma insists upon the limitations of all love short of divine love, and

12 Saint Cecilius is the patron saint of Granada. See JH, 165, for a possible model for this character.

13 *El escultor,* ed. Seco, 43.

14 *Ibid.*

Pedro, who still does not accept God, holds to his original goal of creating his own object of divine love:

> Mas ¿dónde, en qué, mi amor fundo
> si estoy con el Cielo en guerra?
> ¡Creando un Dios en la Tierra,
> para amar en El al mundo! (II, 790)

Upon hearing this sacrilege, Alma flees to the cave in terror and locks herself in.

At the end of the second *auto* Pedro confronts another difficult choice: he can persist in his selfish desire for Alma and his satanic pursuit of self-fulfillment or he can turn away to embrace the divine light, which hovers above the Alhambra. By choosing to persist in his course he chooses to complete his original project: to achieve his own identity at all cost.

The third *auto,* «La muerte,» begins some time later. It is Alma's wedding day and she is dressed in a white bridal gown. Pedro has put on again the sculptor's smock that he wore in the first *auto* and which symbolizes his resumption of his creative quest. Pedro has not yet revealed who he is, but he discloses surprising facts to Alma about herself —that she was illegitimately born in this cave and that her mother unsuccessfully attempted to convert her father to religion. Pedro describes his own wanderings and sufferings and at last reveals who he is: «Y como aguilucho herido... y va a morir a su nido... vuelvo yo a mi edén perdido» (II, 796). He also confesses his intense incestuous love for Alma. She is the dream he has pursued for so many years as he endeavored to create an immortal soul for himself without God's intervention:

> Sí, mi ensueño está en tu rostro,
> y ante mi sueño me postro,
> y adoro al Dios que he creado.
> Ser de mi alma creador,
> crear un alma inmortal
> en mi alma terrenal,
> ser yo mi propio escultor
> con el cincel del dolor;
> sólo, sin Dios, esto fue
> lo que en mis sueños soñé...,
> y ahora que voy a morir,
> despierto y veo surgir
> la escultura de mi fe. (II, 797)

He bows down and humbles himself, adoring the god he imagines he has made —a living sculpture. He begs for a sign of affection from her and says he cares not if he is condemned to burn eternally, as long as he can worship her.

As he reaches for her with lust, Pedro becomes immobilized in a frozen posture at the center of the stage. Alma calls to Aurelio for help, but the only reply is the sound of a shot: Aurelio has committed suicide in despair over having lost Alma. Pedro, by trapping Alma in the cave, has prevented her marriage and put an end to her life as a mortal woman. Because Alma is his immortal soul, his sculpture, she must be freed from the material bonds that enslave and deprive the soul of its immortality. Then, freed at once from his frozen posture and from his lust for Alma, the two are reconciled and fall into a chaste embrace. Pedro kisses her on the forehead and she turns to stone, telling him, «muero en la gloria eterna» (II, 802).

Thus Pedro has completed his sculpture, the God he sought to create. With flageolets sounding in the distance, Pedro pronounces both life and death a «sueño,» no different from the dream embodied in stone. And stating his «esperanza muerta» that death in stone holds greater value than man's existence, he offers to give up his human life « ¡por soñar muerto en la piedra! » (II, 804).[15]

To reflect Pedro's troubled conception of life and death, the stage darkens and Alma disappears behind the curtain at the rear. Pedro clamors for light and Cecilia appears carrying a candle, as she did in the first act. Once more she offers him religious faith, which she says is the light for which he clamors. Man, she tells him, can create things to love, but God alone possesses the divine light by which what we love can be seen. Pedro can share this light if he is worthy, but first he must humble himself and repent on bended knee. If he were to believe, as she does, he would then be able to behold their daughter, whom Cecilia sees in heaven.

But, his pride unbendable, Pedro declares that by force of will he can break the chains that confine him to earth and enter heaven in search of Alma. Snatching a sword from the wall, he cries that he will behead angels, seraphims, archangels, and God himself if they stand in his way. This savage blasphemy convinces Cecilia that her faith is powerless to tame Pedro and that only God's immense goodness can conquer such arrogance. Following Cecilia's plea for divine intervention, the rear curtain opens to reveal a statue of Alma still dressed as a bride and surrounded by an aureole of sanctity. The flageolets sound once more, and the sculptor drops his sword and falls to his knees adoring the statue and symbolically accepting God who has granted him this blessed vision. He exclaims: « ¡Alma! ¡Mi hija!... ¡El ideal!... ¡La fe!... ¡Mi obra maestra! » (II, 808). And then he himself is turned to stone as he states: «Oh, qué ventura es morir / esculpido en forma eterna» (II, 808).

This ambiguous ending raises several questions about Ganivet's intentions and the import of the play. Critics have disagreed over whether a final reconciliation is achieved between the artist and religious faith.[16] But the reconciliation is at best problematic. God remains an unseen accessory to Pedro's self-knowledge, for the vision that Pedro experi-

[15] Shaw has noted the similarity between this and Rubén Darío's poem «Lo fatal,» *The Generation*..., 38. F. García Lorca, *Angel Ganivet*, 43, cites a similarity to the poetry of Antonio Machado.
[16] See note 19 of this chapter.

ences at the end is not a vision of God but of his own completed masterpiece. The statue mirrors a power that was ultimately inside of the artist; divine intervention has only provided a vision of that power. The struggle of the artist to create his final masterpiece has thus been a struggle not with God but with his own muse. The final vision of Alma as «¡El ideal!... ¡La fe!... ¡Mi obra maestra!» therefore represents not so much a religious conversion as the reconciliation of the artist with himself.

This reconciliation, coming after Pedro's return from foreign lands to Spain and to the subterranean chambers in which he had begun his creative activities, suggests that the artist's inspiration was to be found only in his native land, specifically in Granada where the aura of Spain's history can forever nourish him. Just as the path to greatness for Spain, Ganivet never tired of saying, lay within her borders, so the artist's true identity could be achieved only in the heart of his homeland.

Ganivet's insistence on a geographic as well as a cultural centering for the creative imagination brings to mind T. S. Eliot's 1919 essay, «Tradition and the Individual Talent.» Both authors point to the importance of a historical and national perspective from which the individual artist must draw. The following ideas of Eliot show an interesting affinity with the Spanish author:

> ... we shall often find that not only the best, but the most individual parts... [of a poet's] ... work may be those in which the dead poets, his ancestors, assert their immortality... No poet, no artist of any art, has his complete meaning alone. His significance, his appreciation is the appreciation of his relation to the dead poets and artists.[17]

El escultor was first performed in Granada on March 1, 1899, to enormous popular acclaim, according to Francisco Seco de Lucena, who witnessed the event.[18] Yet the work has by no means gained lasting popularity for Ganivet. Dead but a few months at the time when the work was first performed, its enthusiastic reception was due to the public's sympathy for the author rather than the play's intrinsic merit. A number of early critics largely dismissed the play.[19] García Lorca terms its symbols «inefficacious» and states that due to its «tono delirante,» *El escultor* is not representative of Ganivet's work.[20]

But some more recent critics have been kinder. Despite the work's complexity and its awkward attempt to portray spiritual processes in

[17] *Selected Essays of T. S. Eliot,* new ed. (New York, 1950), 4.

[18] «Algo acerca de Ganivet,» 5.

[19] Doris King Arjona, «*La voluntad* and *aboulia* in Contemporary Spanish Ideology», *Revue Hispanique,* LXXIV (1928): 604; Fernández Almagro, *Vida y obra...*, p. 271; César Barja, *Libros y autores contemporáneos,* 36. There are important studies of the work by Hans Jeschke, «Angel Ganivet. Seine Persönlichkeit und Hauptwerke,» *Revue Hispanique,* LXXIV (1928), 228-42; D. L. Shaw, «Ganivet's *El escultor de su alma* —An Interpretation,» *Orbis Litterarum,* XX (1965): 297-306 and in his *The Generation...*, 36-8, and Olmedo Moreno, *El pensamiento de Ganivet,* 270-4.

[20] García Lorca, *Angel Ganivet,* 40, 260.

theatrical form, N. L. Hutman, for instance, has praised its search for forms and symbols suited to the «visión nueva» of modern man's constant «preguntar, negar y dudar.»[21] Yet whatever its virtues as literature, *El escultor* holds a prominent place in Ganivet's works as a compendium of spiritual ideas that had occupied him throughout his career.[22] *El escultor* is therefore Ganivet's last artistic will and testament, just as it is the «tragedy» that Pío Cid tells his friends he will soon leave for them, a drama to take place in the Alhambra which he describes to them as dealing with the «tragedia invariable de la vida» and the «ley primitiva y perenne de la creación» (II, 444).

An incident in Ganivet's life which took place on November 1, 1895, also deserves mention here in the context of *El escultor*'s import as a summation of Ganivet's aesthetic ideas. In a letter to Amelia Roldán of November 3, 1895, Ganivet describes to his mistress his journey to St. Léger, France, where, on All Soul's Day he had his infant daughter reburied and a new gravemarker erected for her (GM: ET, 158-60). The number of similarities between the play and Ganivet's experience three years, almost to the day, earlier are worthy of note. In both cases a father returns to an infant daughter, born out of wedlock, after a lapse of years. In both instances the father feels impelled to return and complete a task that has been left uncompleted or improperly done. Ganivet tells Amelia: «parece que me he quitado un peso de encima» (GM: ET, 160). In both the reburial and the play the task is accomplished underground. The durable results of both tasks are expressed through marble, which is seen as eternal. In the letter Ganivet comments that the letters on the tombstone are on black marble «de modo que no se pierdan nunca», «es una lápida que no se quebrará nunca», «sabemos que si dentro de veinte años volvemos podemos encontrar a la nena como ahora» (GM: ET, 159-60). In both cases the daughter is made eternal, by the marble tombstone and by the marble statue, a work of art which becomes a tombstone both for the daughter and finally for himself. The fact that Ganivet did commit suicide less than three weeks later also suggests that the work had a personal meaning for him that his actions completed, that his life imitated his art and became confused with it.

In writing this «tragedy» Ganivet clearly drew not only on personal issues and the *auto sacramental* of the seventeenth century, but equally on the Spanish Romantic theatre of the nineteenth century, especially on Zorrilla's everlastingly popular *Don Juan Tenorio* (1844). In his rejected 1889 doctoral dissertation *España filosófica contemporánea* he points out that the Romantic movement in the theatre was actually a revival of some of the most characteristic elements of Golden Age drama (II, 606-9), and although he found Romantic theatre quite dead by the late nineteenth century, he wished to connect his creation with traditions that had vitality in Spain and could help renew the national spirit.

[21] «*El escultor de su alma* (La búsqueda de nuevas dimensiones teatrales),» *Papeles de Son Armadans,* XL, 265-6.

[22] Herrero's important interpretation particularly stresses this aspect of the work, JH, 258-60, 248-50, 278-82.

Thus familiar romantic elements such as local color, suicide, forbidden passion, rebelliousness against God, scenes of contrasting light and dark, the quest for freedom from the constraints of society, all give the work a highly romantic cast. And if one notes the use of symbolic statuary and reads the play as an allegory in which Pedro is saved through the intervention of a saintly and pure female figure, then a comparison to the saga of Zorrilla's romantic libertine Don Juan becomes irresistible.

Ganivet's choice of Zorrilla as a model was not random. Zorrilla had been closely identified with Granada during the latter part of his life, and had written an epic poem, *Granada* (1852, left unfinished), retelling Granada's legends up to the Reconquest. He had even been crowned in Granada for his literary achievements in 1889. Ganivet openly admired Zorrilla, calling him Granada's «cantor tradicional» (I, 107). And in *Hombres del norte,* written roughly at the same time as *El escultor,* Ganivet writes that by digging deeply into Spain's historical and popular legends Zorrilla «fue poeta grandísimo» (GM:ET, 31). It is not surprising that Zorrilla's extraordinary theatricality in his reworking of Tirso de Molina's *El burlador de Sevilla y convidado de piedra* (1630) and his interest in Granada should have been in Ganivet's mind when he composed the work that he considered quintessentially Granadan and that he hoped would initiate a theatrical renaissance in his native city. Had he lived longer, Ganivet would have seen his hopes partially fulfilled by Miguel Hernández, Rafael Alberti and Gonzalo Torrente Ballester who followed his lead in turning again to the *auto sacramental* to express their visions of mankind.

At the beginning of November, less than a month after Ganivet completed *El escultor,* his thoughts and behavior began taking on a peculiarity that worried his family and friends. He was terribly agitated, hardly ate, slept, or worked and smoked incessantly, causing a bleeding throat irritation. Letters to his sisters suggest a state of paranoia —Ganivet claimed that he was being pursued and that an Englishman named Powers was the ringleader of an unceasing harrassment. Baron von Brück, the German Consul into whose home Ganivet had moved earlier in the fall, became so disturbed over his colleague's mental perturbation that he persuaded Ganivet to visit Dr. Ottomar van Haken who diagnosed the condition as a progressive general paralysis caused by syphilis, one symptom of which was fantasies of persecution. Hospitalization was considered, but bureaucratic delays, deriving from Ganivet's position as consul, thwarted this hope for medical help.

On November 18 Ganivet sent Navarro Ledesma a postcard informing his friend «atravieso una gran crisis espiritual, que si no estuviera tan bien templado me echaría a la fosa. Por fortuna ya empieza a transformarse en trabajo útil y sano. Si ahora escribiera saldría un ciempiés.»[23]

Ganivet's condition suffered further aggravation about this time with the arrival of an anonymous letter accusing Amelia of infidelity. Another cable arrived soon after from Amelia herself denying the accusation.

[23] «Epistolario,» *Revista de Occidente,* II, no. 33 (1965), 320.

Disturbed by his letters, Amelia borrowed money from Ganivet's sisters and in mid-November she left Spain for Riga, taking Angel Tristán with her. Although Ganivet wrote his family that he was expecting her visit and was looking forward to seeing her, his actions spoke differently.

His depression deepening, on November 27 Ganivet penned a three page document (first published in 1965)[24] addressed to his son, summing up his «ideas y obligaciones.» This was, in effect, Ganivet's apología and last testament to his family. Composed of ten articles, the «Declaración» resembles a Decalogue in which lust, greed, covetousness and false idolatries are proscribed. Some of its entries are logical corollaries to his previously expressed ideas. Others border on the bizarre. And many of his statements carry an apologetic or even defensive tone, as if he were attempting reparation. Defining his own religion as a «misticismo puramente personal,» he states that he has never believed in any «religión positiva» but has respected all religions and never done wrong to any of them. As if to defend himself against unintended wrongdoing, he concedes the negative effects of apparently positive actions and he writes with contrition: «No recuerdo haber hecho mal a nadie siquiera en pensamiento; si hubiera hecho algún mal, pido perdón.»[25] In this vein, and in a reaffirmation of his belief in the possibility of spiritual evolution, he takes a swipe at the moral decadence of his times and holds out at least a frail hope for the future: «Creo que vale más una vida franca y sincera que cien años de hipocresía» he says, and he adds that beneath all hypocrisy there is a natural tendency in man to do good and to experience joy in so doing.[26]

Ganivet also includes some very curious ideas on psychology and eugenics. Although present-day man, he says, lacks spirituality, he should not be destroyed but used to produce a future and more noble being. This transformation can be accomplished through «inventos psicológicos» such as the «cama giratoria,» «zapatos Z,» the «reloj sentimental,» and through diet. It is possible to devise a nutritional system that would reduce the human digestive apparatus and the entire human body to resemble an upright serpent whose bulk would be all brain matter. And to illustrate, Ganivet includes a drawing of this creature which he calls a «Psícope.»[27] (The science fictional quality of these notions recalls the inventions in «Las ruinas de Granada» and an invention in *Los trabajos,* the «luz humana,» which Pío Cid had described to the Duchess of Almadura.)

Ganivet seems here to have lost sight of the distinction between illusion and reality. The «inventions» that lent an air of fantasy and amusement to his fiction become absurd when offered as means for improving human nature and society. They actually carry the ring of madness.

[24] *Ibid.,* 321-3. The document was entrusted to von Brück who was instructed to send it to Navarro Ledesma.
[25] *Ibid.,* 321.
[26] *Ibid.,* 323.
[27] See *ibid.,* 321.

Two days after completing this Declaration, in the early afternoon of November 29, as the ferry crossed the Dvina heading for the center of Riga, Ganivet leaped into the icy river. Although he was rescued and revived by fellow passengers, Ganivet's desire to end his life was not to be thwarted; he immediately plunged into the river again. Efforts to save him were fruitless this time. Amelia had arrived that day and she waited at the consulate in Riga until late in the evening. Doubtless, he did not want to see her because of the reported infidelity, and because of his disturbed condition; his suicide may have been a way of punishing her, but plainly it had more causes than these. He was exhausted from overwork, deteriorating from syphilis, and plagued by chronic and now acute depression. It is also possible that he planned his death as a stoic act, choosing his moment of death with deliberation. In *Los trabajos* he had indicated that death by his own hand was a distinct likelihood, and not a distant one. Whatever the cause, his wounded psyche was unable at last to heal itself through art, love, or religious faith:

¡oh Ganivet
Falto de fe!
¡Lleno de amor
y de dolor!
buzo, buscas, por fin, la misteriosa perla.

RUBÉN DARÍO

CHRONOLOGY

1865	December 13: Angel Ganivet García born in Granada.
1873-1874	The first Spanish Republic.
1874	Restoration of the Bourbon Monarchy, King Alfonso XII proclaimed.
1875	September 4: Death of father, Francisco Ganivet Morcillo.
1876	Seriously injured in a fall.
1877	Leaves school to work in the *notaría* of Abelardo Martínez Contreras.
1880	Begins studies at Instituto de Granada.
1885	June 15: Takes exams for degree of *bachiller* and, on November 27, he competes for the Instituto's *Premio Extraordinario* in Literature, which he is awarded. November 25: Death of Alfonso XII.
1888	Is graduated in June from the University of Granada in Philosophy and Literature. In September he takes an examination for the *Premio Extraordinario* in Philosophy and Literature, which he is subsequently awarded.
1889	March-April: Successfully takes the *oposiciones* for position of *Ayudante* in the *Cuerpo de Archivos, Bibliotecas y Anticuarios.*
1890	March 11: Awarded doctorate in Philosophy and Letters. In June he receives a Bachelor of Law degree from the University of Granada.
1891	Takes competitive exams for chair of Greek at the University of Granada, but is unsuccessful.
1892	February: Meets Amelia Roldán, who will be the mother of his two children, although not his wife. In April and May, he takes the *oposiciones* for a position as vice consul. On May 30 he is named vice consul in Antwerp, Belgium. He takes possession of his post on July 11. Publishes first article «Un festival literario en Amberes» in the newspaper *El Defensor de Granada* 21 August.
1893	February 18: Date of the first letter to Navarro Ledesma which was published posthumously by the recipient in the *Epistolario.* December 11: Birth of his natural daughter, Natalia, in Paris.

1894 February 28: Death of Natalia in Saint Léger les Domart, France.
November 22: Birth of his natural son, Angel Tristán, in Paris.
December 15: Visits Granada where he remains until March, 1895.

1895 January 4: Date of last letter of the Navarro Ledesma *Epistolario,* published posthumously by the recipient.
April 1: Returns to Antwerp.
May 25: Date of his first letter to Nicolás María López, published posthumously by recipient in *La Cofradía del Avellano.*
August 16: Death of his mother, Doña María de los Angeles García Siles in Granada. Ganivet makes a short visit to Granada, returning to Antwerp in early September.
In November, he visits Paris.
On December 20 he finishes the novel, *La conquista del reino de Maya por el último conquistador español, Pío Cid.*
December 25: He is promoted to consul, second class, in Helsinki.

1896 January 31: Arrives in Helsinki.
February 14: He begins to write the essays comprising *Granada la bella* which he finishes on February 27. They are first published in *El Defensor de Granada.*
July 10: Published «El arte español juzgado en el extranjero.»
In September *Granada la bella* is published in Helsinki in book form. In October he finishes *Idearium español.*

1897 Finishes *Cartas finlandesas.*
Spends June-September in Spain.
On July 7, the writers of Granada sponsor a banquet there in his honor.
In August the Spanish Prime Minister Antonio Cánovas del Castillo is assassinated by an anarchist.

1898 January 26: Sends «Jonas Lie» first article of series *Hombres del norte.*
February 4: Death of Ganivet's maternal grandfather, Francisco de Paula García Hurtado.
Spanish defeated by the United States at Cavite, Philippines, May 1, and Santiago de Cuba, July 3.
June 8: Named Spanish consul in Riga, Latvia, a post he assumes August 10.
9-15 July, and 6-14 September: his contributions to a public exchange of letters with Miguel de Unamuno appear in *El Defensor de Granada.* (The first complete book edition of this correspondence is published as *El porvenir de España* in 1912.)
In September, his *Cartas finlandesas* appears in book form.
In May and October, the two volumes of the novel *Los tra-*

bajos del infatigable creador, Pío Cid are published in Madrid. November 11: Ganivet sends the manuscript of his play *El escultor de su alma* to Granada.
On November 29, he drowns himself in the Dvina River.
December 10: The Treaty of Paris is signed by representatives of Spain and the United States by which Spain loses Cuba, Puerto Rico, Guam and the Philippines.

SELECTED BIBLIOGRAPHY

PRIMARY SOURCES

Obras completas de Angel Ganivet (Madrid: Aguilar, 1943, 2nd ed., 1959; 3rd ed., 1961).

NOVELS

La conquista del reino de Maya por el último conquistador español, Pío Cid (Madrid: Sucesores de Rivadeneyra, 1897).

Los trabajos del infatigable creador, Pío Cid (Madrid: Sucesores de Rivadeneyra, 1898).

ESSAYS

Cartas finlandesas de Angel Ganivet, cónsul de España en Helsinfors (Granada: Viuda e Hijos de Sabatel, 1898), Private Edition, with a prologue, «Ganivet y sus obras,» by Nicolás María López.

España filosófica contemporánea y otros trabajos (Madrid: Librería Francisco Beltrán y Victoriano Suárez, 1930), vol. IX of *Obras completas de Angel Ganivet.*

Granada la bella (Helsinki: J. C. Frenckell and Son, 1896).

Granada la bella, por Angel Ganivet (Granada: Editorial Padre Suárez, 1954), edited and a prologue by Antonio Gallego y Burín.

Hombres del norte y Artículos varios (Granada: El Defensor de Granada, 1905), with a prologue by Rafael Gago Palomo.

Hombres del norte. El porvenir de España (Madrid: Victoriano Suárez, 1905), edited by Angel T. de Ganivet.

Idearium español (Granada: Viuda e Hijos de Paulino V. Sabatel, 1897).

El porvenir de España, co-authored with Miguel de Unamuno (Madrid: Renacimiento, 1912).

Other editions of these works are given in ANTONIO GALLEGO MORELL, *Estudios y textos ganivetianos* (Madrid: Consejo Superior de Investigaciones, 1971), 183-6.

CORRESPONDENCE

La Cofradía del Avellano: Cartas de Angel Ganivet (Granada: Luis F. Pinar Rocha, 1935), edited and with a prologue by NICOLÁS MARÍA LÓPEZ.

Correspondencia familiar de Angel Ganivet: 1888-1897 (Granada: Anel, 1967), edited and with an introduction and notes by JAVIER HERRERO.

Epistolario (Madrid: Biblioteca Nacional y Extranjera, 1904), with a prologue by F. NAVARRO LEDESMA.

Juicio de Angel Ganivet sobre su obra literaria (Cartas inéditas) (Granada: Universidad de Granada, 1962), edited and with a prologue by LUIS SECO DE LUCENA Y PAREDES.

For a listing of other published letters that do not comprise an entire volume see A. GALLEGO MORELL, *Estudios y textos ganivetianos,* 188. The unpublished correspondence between Ganivet and Navarro Ledesma is in the possession of the Hispanic Society of America in New York City.

PLAY

El escultor de su alma. Drama místico en tres actos compuesto por Angel Ganivet (Granada: El Defensor de Granada, 1904), with a prologue by FRANCISCO SECO DE LUCENA.

ARTICLES AND SKETCHES NOT INCORPORATED IN *Obras completas* OR IN ANY OF THE ABOVE

«Academia de los nocturnos,» *Boletín del Centro Artístico* (2.ª época), Granada, 1915, Núm. 4, 2-3.
«El cabeza de familia,» *Boletín del Centro Artístico* (2.ª época), Granada, 1915, Núm. 4, 2-3.
«Epílogo que puede servir de prólogo,» in A. GALLEGO MORELL, *Estudios y textos ganivetianos* (Madrid: Consejo Superior de Investigaciones, 1971), 36-8.
«Un festival literario en Amberes,» *El Defensor de Granada,* 21 agosto 1892.
«Una idea,» *El Defensor de Granada,* 26 octubre 1898.
«Mis inventos (La imagen muscular),» *Vida Nueva,* Madrid, Núm. 30, 1 enero 1899.
«El mundo soy yo o el hombre de las dos caras,» with a preliminary note by Hans Jeschke, *La Gaceta Literaria,* Madrid, 1928, Núm. 46, 1.
«¡Nañññ!...,» *Vida Nueva,* Madrid, núm. 19, 16 octubre 1898.
«Nuestro espíritu misterioso,» *El Defensor de Granada,* 16 septiembre 1898.
«El progreso material,» *El Defensor de Granada,* 16 diciembre 1898.
«Rêveur,» in A. GALLEGO MORELL, *Estudios y textos ganivetianos* (Madrid: Consejo Superior de Investigaciones, 1971), 39-41.

SECONDARY SOURCES

1. BIBLIOGRAPHIES

ANTONIO GALLEGO MORELL: *Estudios y textos ganivetianos* (Madrid: Consejo Superior de Investigaciones, 1971), 183-214.

2. BOOKS

AGUDIEZ, JUAN V.: *Las novelas de Angel Ganivet* (New York: Anaya, 1972).
ALVAREZ, A.: *The Savage God: A Study of Suicide* (New York: Random House, 1961).
AZAÑA, MANUEL: *Obras completas* (México: Oasis, 1966), 3 vols.
BADINTER, ELIZABETH: *Mother Love: Myth and Reality* (New York: MacMillan, 1981).
BARJA, CÉSAR: *Libros y autores contemporáneos* (New York: Las Américas, 1964, 2nd ed.).
BLANCO AGUINAGA, CARLOS: *Juventud del 98* (Madrid: Siglo XXI, 1970).
BRENAN, GERALD: *The Spanish Labyrinth* (Oxford: Oxford U.P., 1954).

FERNÁNDEZ ALMAGRO, MELCHOR: *Vida y obra de Angel Ganivet* (Madrid: Revista de Occidente, 1952, 2nd ed.).
GALLEGO MORELL, ANTONIO: *Angel Ganivet, el excéntrico del 98* (Madrid: Guadarrama, 1974).
GARCÍA LORCA, FRANCISCO: *Angel Ganivet, su idea del hombre* (Buenos Aires: Losada, 1952).
HERRERO, JAVIER: *Angel Ganivet, un iluminado* (Madrid: Gredos, 1966).
JAMES, SELWIN: *South of the Congo* (New York: Random House, 1943).
LAÍN ENTRALGO, PEDRO: *España como problema* (Madrid: Aguilar, 1957).
LITVAK, LILY: *A Dream of Arcadia: Anti-Industrialism in Spanish Literature* (Austin and London: University of Texas Press, 1975).
LÓPEZ MORILLAS, JUAN: *Hacia el 98: literatura, sociedad, ideología* (Barcelona: Ariel, 1972).
OLMEDO MORENO, MIGUEL: *El pensamiento de Angel Ganivet* (Madrid: Revista de Occidente, 1965).
RAMSDEN, HERBERT: *Angel Ganivet's 'Idearium español': A Critical Study* (Manchester: University of Manchester, 1967).
— *The 1898 Movement in Spain: Towards a Reinterpretation with Special Referente to «En torno al casticismo» and «Idearium español»* (Manchester: University of Manchester Press, 1974).
SCANLON, GERALDINE: *La polémica feminista en la España contemporánea: 1868-1974* (Madrid: Siglo XXI de España, 1976).
SOBEJANO, GONZALO: *Nietzsche en España* (Madrid: Gredos, 1967).
SHAW, DONALD L.: *The Generation of 1898 in Spain* (London: Ernest Benn, 1975).
ZULUETA, CARMEN DE: *Navarro Ledesma, el hombre y su tiempo* (Madrid: Alfaguara, 1968).

3. ARTICLES

AGUDIEZ, JUAN V.: «Ganivet en las huellas de Galdós y Alarcón,» *Nueva Revista de Filología Hispánica,* año XVI, núms. 1-2 (1962), 89-95.
— «Angel Ganivet y su correspondencia inédita con Francisco Navarro Ledesma», *Nueva Revista de Filología Hispánica,* 21 (1972), 338-62.
ALDARACA, BRIDGET: «El ángel del hogar: The Cult of Domesticity in Nineteenth-Century Spain,» *Theory and Practice of Feminist Literary Criticism,* eds. Gabriela Mora and Karen Van Hooft (Ypsilanti, Michigan: Bilingual Press, 1982), 62-87.
CASALDUERO, JOAQUÍN: «Descripción del problema de la muerte en Angel Ganivet,» *Bulletin Hispanique,* XXXIII (1931), 214-46.
— «Ganivet en el camino,» *Bulletin Hispanique,* XXXVI (1934), 488-99.
CASTRO VILLACAÑAS, DEMETRIO: «Angel Ganivet, su contradicción,» *Clavileño,* XXV (1954), 49-54.
CONRADI, GUSTAV A.: «El ideal de la indiferencia creadora en Angel Ganivet,» *Arbor,* XXXII (1955), 1-20.
DURÁN, MANUEL: «Ganivet y el senequismo hispánico,» *Insula,* 228-9 (1965), 3, 19.
FRANCO, JEAN: «Ganivet and the Technique of Satire in *La conquista del reino de Maya,*» *Bulletin of Hispanic Studies,* XLII (1965), 34-44.
FUENTES, VÍCTOR: «Creación y estética en Ganivet,» *Revista Hispánica Moderna,* XXXI (1965), 133-41.
GALLEGO MORELL, ANTONIO: «Poemas en francés de Angel Ganivet,» *Revista de Occidente,* XI (1965), 356-68.
GÓMEZ MORENO, MANUEL: «Recuerdos de un condiscípulo,» *Revista de Occidente,* XI (1965), 324-30.

HERRERO, JAVIER: «Ganivet y su canciller en Amberes,» *Revista Hispánica Moderna,* XXX (1964), 271-8.

— «El elemento biográfico en *Los trabajos de Pío Cid,*» *Hispanic Review,* XXXIV (1966), 95-116.

— «Spain as Virgin: Radical Traditionalism in Angel Ganivet,» *Homenaje a Juan López-Morillas,* eds. JOSÉ AMOR Y VÁZQUEZ and A. DAVID KOSSOFF (Madrid: Gredos, 1982, 247-256.

HUTMAN, NORMA L.: «*El escultor de su alma* (La búsqueda de nuevas dimensiones teatrales),» *Papeles de Son Armadans,* XI, 265-84.

JESCHKE, HANS: «Angel Ganivet. Seine Persönlichkeit und Hauptwerke,» *Revue Hispanique,* LXXII (1982), 102-246.

KING ARONJA, DORIS: «*La voluntad* and *abulia* in Contemporary Spanish Ideology,» *Revue Hispanique,* LXXIV (1928), 573-672.

LAFFRANQUE, MARIE: «A propos de *Lourdes* d'Emile Zola: Angel Ganivet et le christianisme contemporain,» *Bulletin Hispanique,* LXIX (1967), 56-84.

— «Angel Ganivet y el ocaso de la filosofía greco-romana,» *Insula,* 228-9 (1965), 6-7.

— «L'inspiration stoicienne chez Angel Ganivet,» *Caravelle,* VI (1966), 5-31.

MARAVALL, JOSÉ ANTONIO: «Ganivet y el tema de la autenticidad nacional,» *Revista de Occidente,* XI, no. 33 (1965), 389-409.

MARICHAL, JUAN: «Ideas picudas, ideas redondas: Maupassant y Ganivet,» *Nueva Revista de Filología Hispánica,* VIII (1954), 77-9.

— «Dos lectures de Ganivet: 1937, 1965,» *Papeles de Son Armadans,* XL, 245-51.

MONTES HUIDOBRO, MATÍAS: «El dogma de la Inmaculada Concepción como interpretación de la mujer en la obra de Ganivet,» *Duquesne Hispanic Review,* 13 (1968), 9-25.

— «*Cartas finlandesas:* Ganivet, agonista de la percepción y del lenguaje,» *Revista de Estudios Hispánicos,* X (1976), 3-30.

OSBORNE, ROBERT E.: «Observations on Ganivet's *La conquista del reino de Maya,*» *Homenaje a Rodríguez-Moñino* (Madrid: Castalia, 1966), I, 39-45.

PARKER, ALEXANDER A.: «The Novels of Ganivet,» *Homenaje a Juan López-Morillas,* eds. JOSÉ AMOR and A. DAVID KOSSOF (Madrid: Gredos, 1982), 369-382.

RICARD, ROBERT: «Deux romanciers: Ganivet et Galdós. Affinités et oppositions,» *Bulletin Hispanique,* LX (1958), 484-99.

ROS GARCÍA, JUAN: «Los caminos del ensayo: Ganivet y las *Cartas finlandesas,*» *Estudios literarios dedicados al Profesor Mariano Baquero Goyanes,* ed. VICTORINO POLO GARCÍA (Murcia, 1974), 452-4.

SENABRE, RICARDO: «Ganivet y el diagnóstico de la abulia,» *Studia hispánica in honorem R. Lapesa* (Madrid: Gredos, 1972), 595-599.

SERRANO PONCELA, SEGUNDO: «Ganivet en sus cartas,» *Revista Hispánica Moderna,* XXIV (1958), 301-11.

SHAW, DONALD L.: «Ganivet's *España filosófica contemporánea* and the Interpretation of the Generation of 1898,» *Hispanic Review,* XXVIII (1960), 220-32.

— «Ganivet's *El escultor de su alma:* an Interpretation,» *Orbis litterarum,* XX (1965), 297-306.

SHAW, K. E.: «Angel Ganivet: a Sociological Interpretation,» *Revista de Estudios Hispánicos,* 11 (1968), 165-181.

SOBEJANO, GONZALO: «Ganivet o la soberbia,» *Cuadernos Hispano-americanos,* 35 (1958), 133-57.

SORIA, ANDRÉS: «Ganivet, el escritor,» *Insula,* 228-29 (1965), 11.

WONDER, JOHN P.: «Angel Ganivet and the Study of Language,» *Romance Notes,* 11 (1969), 82-88.